W9-AFX-163

Merv Griffin's Crosswords Pocket Volume 3

100 Easy-to-Hard Crossword Puzzles

Edited by
Timothy Parker

St. Martin's Paperbacks

MERV GRIFFIN'S CROSSWORDS POCKET VOLUME 3

Copyright © 2008 by Merv Griffin Enterprises.

Cover photo of Merv Griffin © Merv Griffin Entertainment. Cover photo of Ty Treadway © Aaron Rapoport.

ISBN: 0-312-94700-3
EAN: 978-0-312-94700-2

Printed in the United States of America

St. Martin's Paperbacks edition / January 2008

St. Martin's Paperbacks are published by St. Martin's Press, 175 Fifth Avenue, New York, NY 10010.

10 9 8 7 6 5 4 3 2 1

Merv Griffin's
Crosswords
Pocket
Volume 3

TAKE YOUR TEMPERATURE

ACROSS

1 Chief monk
6 Piano exercise
11 Racer's relative
14 Capital near Alexandria
15 House components
16 Seashell seller
17 Showed trepidation
19 Lion or Tiger
20 Slalom path
21 Downhill racer
22 Completely unfamiliar
24 Jocular Johnson
25 Burly
26 Gangster's weapon
29 Fleming characters
31 Poetry Muse
32 Hood
33 Bit of mosaic
37 Lost one's temper
40 Responds in "Jeopardy!"
41 Eye of ___ (part of a "Macbeth" recipe)
42 Be fearful of
43 City near Brigham City
45 Lengthy recitation
46 Old hags
49 Granola ingredients
50 Fastener for Rosie
51 Cookie sheetful
53 Follow a Vail trailp

56 Gardner of Hollywood
57 Compassionate
60 Scuff up, e.g.
61 Rub out
62 Herman's Hermits lead singer
63 Layer
64 Bocelli's pitch
65 "Nifty!"

DOWN

1 Feel pain
2 Utters, like a sheep
3 Contractors' offers
4 Tolkien creature
5 Machine shop area
6 Marsh growth
7 Java joint
8 State with conviction
9 "Jungle Fever" director
10 What you will
11 Jellied garnish
12 Ogre of note
13 Flashy flower
18 Mandolin cousin
23 Skills of yesterday
24 Display unity
25 Lovelorn's utterance
26 Country's McEntire
27 Cinnabar, taconite, etc.
28 Potato holder
29 Displayed
30 Masters' stroke

Puzzle 1

32 Archaic pronoun
34 Invention beginning
35 Mean partner
36 Little whirlpool
38 Drops the curtain on
39 Lily Tomlin character
44 Jump in the pool
45 "Arsenic and Old ___"
46 Swimmer's bane
47 Romantic competitor
48 Part of a floral carpel
49 It may be just past significant
51 Fiber source
52 "Are not!" retort
53 Promenade
54 Superman, most often
55 Lead-in for gram or graph
58 Were now?
59 Lobster coral

EXTREMITIES

ACROSS

1 Naples staple
6 "___ Me Nearer"
10 Churchill's "___ Country"
14 Out of round
15 Justice cover-up?
16 It may climb the walls
17 Like a fat cat
19 "Bus Stop" playwright
20 Neatened the lawn, in a way
21 Blew a gasket
22 Architectural tapers
25 Metric capacity units
26 Angel's abode
27 "Stand By Me" director
29 Waits at the light
30 Calabash
31 Women's ___
34 Some black sheep
35 Plants considered as a group
36 SNL's Carvey
37 Naval Academy grad. (Abbr.)
38 System of principles
39 Creator
40 Gussies up
42 Passenger ships
43 Walked purposefully
45 Least foolish
46 Reprimand mildly
47 Fine-feathered specimen
49 1968 Nobel Peace Prize winner Cassin

50 Rodgers and Hart musical
55 Where to see Puppis and Carina
56 Baltimore's McHenry, for one
57 Au courant
58 Dinner at boot camp
59 Drifting ice
60 Oscar winner Sophia

DOWN

1 "Batman" sound
2 "___ Maria"
3 The sun, to Seneca
4 "___ death do us . . ."
5 Cleaves
6 Bottom-of-the-barrel stuff
7 Thespian's gig
8 Reading position, often
9 Tie the knot
10 Emulate Wiley Post
11 Region of New York
12 Get one's dander up
13 Wind instruments
18 First family's address?
21 Coat you throw away without regret
22 Coupe alternative
23 California resort city
24 Burl of film and song
25 One-time Venetian coin
26 Engage one's services

Puzzle 2

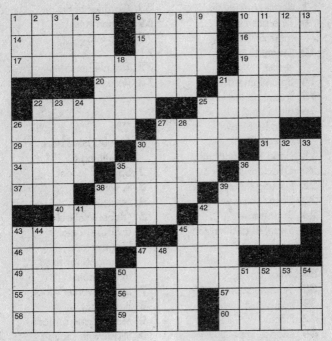

27 Crucifixes
28 Mark alternative
30 "Glengarry ___ Ross"
32 Not active
33 Denies access to
35 Able to act at will
36 Great dog
38 Yield, as property
39 Dry, cold northerly wind
41 Cowboy competitions
42 In ___ of (replacing)
43 "Shoo!"

44 When repeated,
a comforting phrase
45 Corresponded
47 Organic compound
48 Greek diner order
50 Inaccurate
51 Quarter of eight
52 Regatta implement
53 Old syllable
meaning "before"
54 Fractional monetary
unit of Japan

AQUATIC FUN

ACROSS

1 Some cantata singers
6 Fine-grained mineral
10 "Want to hear a secret?"
14 Small hand drum
15 Truant, in the USMC
16 Blues singer James
17 It doesn't leave a paper trail
18 Linda Ronstadt hit
20 Olfactory stimuli
22 Parking lot topper
23 Hosp. employee
24 Brainstorm
26 Sweetest and kindest
28 Bobby Darin hit
33 It could be stuffed
34 Actor Erwin
35 Stadium sounds
39 Fall, while surfing
42 Finch
44 Glance impolitely
45 U.S.A. defense agency
47 Diamond-studded topper
48 Part of an Otis Redding hit
52 Puget Sound city
55 Combat for two
56 Familiar vow
57 Exist
59 Footwear giant
63 Henry Mancini hit

66 Got into pitch
68 Gardner of fiction
69 Roman ruler
70 Step into
71 Lull
72 Trouble persistently
73 Pitiless

DOWN

1 "It must have been something I ___!"
2 Spiritual leader
3 A winter lift
4 Miscellanea
5 "Rebel Without a Cause" actor
6 Programmed command for fixed indentations
7 Leatherworker's tool
8 Big galoot
9 Makes quite a profit
10 Word with "soup" or "shooter"
11 Vogue
12 F3.5 and F4.0
13 Reproach bitterly
19 It's cheesy
21 Cookbook direction
25 Patient sounds?
27 King novel
28 Big sports event
29 Peace Nobelist Wiesel
30 "Oh, my!"
31 Strain one's muscles

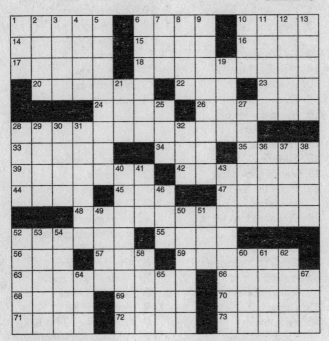

32 Toy store aliens
36 League type
37 Israeli dance
38 Oscillate
40 Not concerned
41 "For shame!"
43 They participate
in big games
46 Icelander's catch
49 Tent tycoon
50 Plow line
51 Start of a giggle

52 Official recorder
53 Hold precious
54 Chills
58 Free from fluctuations
60 It can be a drag
61 Understanding
62 Quick-witted
64 Spiker's barrier
65 Historic time
67 Unbuttered

TRICKY, TRICKY

ACROSS

1 Concerning the ear
5 They can be programmed
9 Four-flusher
14 Literally "I am unwilling"
15 Quaker State port
16 Mend the lawn
17 ___ the Red
18 Preakness entries
20 Swindles
22 Waste allowance
23 Prefix for field or stream
24 Response to a weak joke, perhaps
27 Clown's prop
30 OB-GYN's org.
33 Habitations at high altitudes
35 Anger
36 Words with "pour" or "pass"
37 Swindles
40 Seth's son
41 Vitiate
42 Literary ridicule
43 Domestic retreat
44 Khartoum's country
46 Word with common or horse
47 Frazier or Friday
48 Doing business
50 Swindles
56 What some speculate in
57 "American ___"
59 Make a change
60 Wee thing
61 Bad thing to be under
62 Some stingers
63 Telescope part
64 Sasquatch's kin

DOWN

1 Beatles collection
2 Cause for civil action
3 Operatic Trojan princess
4 Some mixed drinks
5 Biblical unit
6 Arts companion
7 "Miami Vice" cop
8 Farsighted one?
9 Loss's opposite
10 Judean king, 37-4 B.C.
11 ___ buco (veal shanks)
12 December song
13 QB's gain or loss
19 Small villages
21 Bald eagle's cousins
24 Displayed a big mouth?
25 Go back to school, in a way
26 Sweater material
28 Coronation coronet
29 It's so taxing!
30 Ordered out

Puzzle 4

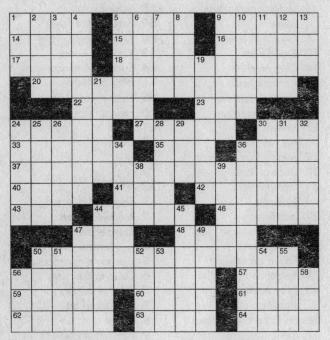

31 Peatlands
32 Parisian's year
34 Clemens and Gompers
36 Grow stronger
38 It's all the craze
39 Desert meccas
44 Detoxifies (with "up")
45 Carney's "Honeymooners" role
47 Mint ___
49 They rhyme with reason

50 Boxer Oscar ___ Hoya
51 Nosebag filler
52 Bibliographer's abbr.
53 Oscar nominee Blanchett
54 Falco who plays Carmela
55 Put into piles
56 Like steak tartare
58 Lanai necklace

MOO!

ACROSS

1 Heavy construction piece
6 Give it all away
10 Bread woe
14 Comaneci, of Olympic fame
15 Istanbul currency
16 Cherbourg chum
17 Where you'll get cold comfort
19 Middle East hot spot
20 Soak a fiber
21 Consent from Chirac
22 Sub head
24 Checks for ages, say
25 Wood file
27 Fail to go straight
28 Target of many a line
33 Lofty Anchorage sighting
36 End of a break, often
37 Skin
38 Nerve fiber
39 CD displacer
40 Verve
41 Hightailed it
42 "The Matrix" hero
43 Most skilled
45 "Yikes!"
48 Moving machine part
49 Monday's crossword, compared to Friday's
50 Mountain pass
53 Fiendishly wicked
57 Quintana ___
58 Before
59 Serengeti resident
60 Obsequious person
63 Arbuckle pooch
64 Spanish-American War battleship
65 Thick piece
66 Hair spiffers
67 Zenith
68 Deserted

DOWN

1 Short-tailed lemur
2 Bellowed bleats
3 Bowdlerizes
4 ___ Jordan
5 Like some city races
6 Close to the color of the sky
7 Bald-faced bit
8 Sector
9 First aid staple
10 It may be cast
11 Actor Sharif
12 Judy's daughter
13 Do business
18 To some degree
23 It gives you inside info
26 Irritate
28 Some stocking stuffers
29 Wrap up
30 Account
31 History periods?

32 Utilize and return
33 Verve
34 Northern major-leaguer
35 Oft-repeated carol word
39 End of the fourth qtr., typically
42 It used to be South West Africa
43 Fulfillment of a burning desire?

44 Destiny's Child singer
46 Hipster's interjection
47 Sound blocker
50 Fill the tank
51 Author's promoter
52 Daffy pal
53 Wade through mud
54 ___-de-camp
55 Labor
56 Cut corners?
61 Be in the red
62 Physics unit

TAKE OFF!

ACROSS

1 "Speed" speeder
4 Slugger Jim
9 Quibbles
14 Big item in Hollywood?
15 Beau
16 Pacific greeting
17 "Enough!"
20 Living room furniture piece
21 Like loafers
22 Actor Cobb
23 Lake Ontario port
26 "Citizen Kane" studio
29 Show fallibility
30 More cunning
31 Iron clothes
32 Ascend
33 Snoopy, for one
35 Entertainment apparatus
38 Conquer partner
39 Dostoevsky subject
40 Wet blanket
41 Kwajalein is one
42 Shad delicacy
45 Koppel of "Nightline"
46 Discussion groups
48 Lima's land
49 Utopias
51 Windshield apparatus
52 "Almost finished!"
57 Indy driver
58 Old anesthetic
59 Conciliatory gesture
60 Prefix meaning "wind"
61 ___ Island
62 Chicago-to-Detroit dir.

DOWN

1 Church of England officer
2 Like the wicked stepsisters vis-a-vis Cinderella
3 Crossword tackler
4 Double
5 Monopolize
6 "I'm impressed!"
7 Ran into
8 Pencil topper
9 Monte ___
10 Nautical direction
11 Driver's control problem
12 High degree
13 For example
18 British rule in India
19 Journal
23 Popeye's girl
24 ___ Valley, Calif.
25 Internet area
27 Tartan garb
28 "Bravo!"
30 Iditarod vehicle
31 It's rigged
32 Football foul

33 Brings water to
   212 degrees
34 Carbon compound
35 Pirelli product
36 Forensic material
37 Second Commandment
   taboo
38 Banned pesticide
41 Correct reply
42 Tranquillity
43 Crater Lake site
44 Second smallest continent

46 Pitcher Martinez
47 "It's ___-win situation!"
48 Fruit center, perhaps
50 Judge
51 "If I ___ a Carpenter"
52 Second Amendment
   lobby
53 007 creator Fleming
54 Ultimate degree
55 Expression of surprise
56 "Waking ___
   Devine" (1998)

FOLLOW THE RULES

ACROSS

1 "Call me ___"
   (Hope film)
6 "What a pity!"
10 Strike breaker
14 Ticks off
15 Type of defense
16 Glee club member
17 International
   holdup man?
18 Wedding cake layer
19 Word with base
   or summer
20 By any means
23 Rumanian coin
24 Congenial
25 No so great
28 Polished off
29 Gangster's gun
30 TV actress Charlotte
31 Not yet solidified
34 Kind of alert
36 Scholarly book
37 However one can
40 Oracle's sign
41 Ultimatum word
42 Delineates
43 Go ___ (freak out)
44 Uh-huh
45 Someone or
   something special
46 Give a pounding
48 Molecule piece
50 Pressure unit
53 Without constraint
56 Exploitive fellow
58 Light green legume
59 Stocking shade
60 Musical pause
61 Arab ruler
62 Nepal's neighbor
63 Org. with missions
64 Elbow benders
65 Advantageous
   purchase

DOWN

1 Donnybrook
2 Slender branch
3 Reduce, as fears
4 Full-strength,
   as a drink
5 Give one's
   approval for
6 People conquered
   by Cortes
7 French wine
   valley and river
8 In a fresh way
9 Blood bank
   science
10 Gives the axe
11 Teacher's milieu
12 Bread machine?
13 Monk's style
21 Engage in a contest
22 Warning hue
26 Ireland's De Valera
27 Smells awful
28 Eternity
29 Friar's attire

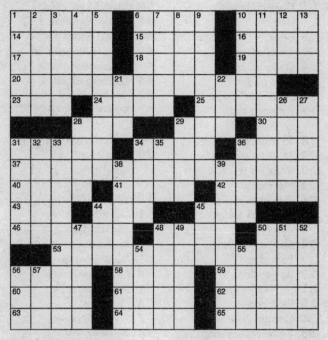

31 WWII predator
32 Insect larva
33 Transparent quality
34 Flatfish
35 Bride's new title
36 Even off
38 Peepers' places
39 Ornamental
flowering vine
44 Cinder
45 Old salt
47 Heart line

48 Own up to
49 Some past despots
50 Goody-goody
51 Rich brown pigment
52 Standard of
perfection
54 VIP transport
55 Babble angrily
56 Footed vase
57 Bounding main

PAIR OF TWOS

ACROSS

1 German family member
5 Bossa ___
9 "Avalon" author
14 Doctor's advice
15 Steel girder
16 "Rawhide" singer
17 Put one's chips on the table?
18 To a smaller extent
19 Think alike
20 Wedded pair
23 Net receipt?
24 Physics particles
25 "Baseball Tonight" network
28 She played Laurie Partridge
29 Be beholden to
31 ___ Paulo, Brazil
33 Tic-tac-toe winner
34 Cowgirl Dale
36 Protective covering
38 Quiet business associate
42 Part of a play
43 Evidence of cooking
44 Herd word
45 Afternoon affair
48 Type of liner
49 It's pressed for cash
52 First name in mysteries
54 Jazzy Fitzgerald
56 Turf starter
58 Certain look-alike
61 Garden gastropod
63 On the apex
64 Word with vapor or combination
65 Camping digs
66 Hardly genteel
67 Sal the mule's canal
68 Out
69 Earned a citation
70 "I guess so"

DOWN

1 Like mirrors and windows
2 Appellative change
3 Away from the good
4 Development areas?
5 Sight in Memphis
6 Compliant
7 ___ da Gama
8 Illegal firings?
9 Stick starter
10 Two below par
11 Tedious
12 Penultimate word in a countdown
13 Part of an extended name
21 "What a great gift!"
22 Patriotic shout
26 Flimsy, as an excuse
27 Neither counterpart
30 Pallid

Puzzle 8

32 Kind of cookie
34 Wallach, for one
35 Treadmill site
37 Genetic messenger letters
38 "The Lion King" character
39 Pisa residents
40 Three-digit number
41 Singer Orbison
42 Lincoln's nickname
46 Velvet ender

47 Religious platforms
49 On the job
50 Nixon's daughter
51 Business beginner
53 Corrects copy
55 Illuminated
57 Pope of the fifth century
59 Apart from this
60 Did a Little bit?
61 NASCAR advertiser
62 Class-conscious org.?

SEASON'S GREETINGS

ACROSS

1 Anchorman's summary
6 Protozoa propellers, perhaps
11 Rock's Rose
14 Romantic entanglement
15 Tip over
16 Oscar role for Field
17 SUMMER
19 Rambler's word
20 Prior to
21 Veggie discard
22 More than a dash, briefly
23 Scott Joplin tune
24 Outback discoveries
26 Vocation
28 FALL
33 Sidestep
34 Pretend
35 Halloween decorations
36 Dilapidated
38 Word with bag or box
42 Rockies resort
44 Termite, for one
45 WINTER
50 Ekberg of "La Dolce Vita"
51 "Oh my gosh!"
52 Soldier material
53 Jet setting
56 ___ Grande
57 Spot's sound
60 Colorado Indian
61 SPRING
64 Sleep stage
65 Comic Kovacs
66 Conjure up
67 Proposed change to the Const.
68 Equestrian's pride
69 Called

DOWN

1 Talk like Froggy
2 Abu Dhabi honcho
3 Sprinkle site
4 Cal. abbreviation
5 Stylishly dressed student
6 Snuggle
7 Wall St. intro
8 Contributed temporarily
9 Lodgings
10 Become fit for
11 Genesis mountainous region
12 Site of Kubla Khan's pleasure dome
13 Cliff dwelling locales
18 Mottled horse
24 Sea dog
25 Hush
27 Coerced payments
28 Condensation
29 Time to celebrate
30 It'll give you a fare deal
31 Flanders on "The Simpsons"

Puzzle 9

32 Shoat's home
36 Spot for a rubdown
37 "Black as ___ was crow"
39 Leon Uris hero
40 Big-top safety precaution
41 Liquor-free
43 Spirited meetings?
44 Black cat, to some
45 Word with human or Mother
46 Minister, at times

47 Fellini's medium
48 Saw eye to eye
49 "The best ___ plans . . ."
54 Military structure
55 Pedigree
57 Microscopic bit
58 Get rid of some dead wood
59 Took off
62 Dishonest response
63 Zsa Zsa's sister

SAY WHAT?

ACROSS

1 Weakens, as support
5 Treat for Cookie Monster
10 Pack gently
14 Hoodwink
15 Bakery lure
16 Above
17 Approach the gate
18 Businesses
19 Spanish surrealist
20 Madison and Lincoln, e.g.
23 Reason for a shot in the arm?
25 Boat's stopover
26 Beneficiary
27 Brisk
29 Senior celebration
31 Speedy delivery
35 Blubber
38 Stink big-time
39 Some oilmen
40 Fashion magazine
41 Be human, so they say
42 18th Amendment outgrowths
44 Opponent for Andre
45 Ditto!
46 One place to roll in
49 Forefather
52 FDR's successor
53 Baloney!
57 Campus sports org.
58 Cropped up
59 Important stretches of time
62 "Now hear ___"
63 South Korea's capital
64 Apportion
65 New Year's word
66 Great expectations
67 Inkling

DOWN

1 Young newt
2 Constrictor, e.g.
3 Church meal, perhaps
4 Buttonhole, e.g.
5 Floats through the air
6 Israel's Sharon
7 Military might
8 Oscar-winning Thompson
9 Grating sound
10 Hand-beaten drum
11 Birdlike
12 Haggard songwriter?
13 The written word
21 Hand lender
22 Matinee is one kind
23 "___ Jacques"
24 Less strict
28 Annoy
29 Monopoly place
30 Shine's partner
32 Mo. for sapphires
33 Barrie bad guy

34 She played
 Rosemary
35 Emulated a snake
36 Spreads on breads
37 Ply with drink
40 Legal conclusion?
42 Tiresias, for one
43 Pre-meal word, perhaps
44 Gratify
46 Cousin providers
47 Like some
 trigger fingers

48 Laundry problem
49 Eavesdropper
50 Magazine
 installment
51 Staggers
54 "A Beautiful
 Mind" subject
55 Treat for Cookie
 Monster
56 Big rig
60 Partook of
61 Kind of horse

GET BUSY

ACROSS

1 "Let's not forget . . ."
5 Urban oasis
9 Swahili boss
14 Carson's Carnac, e.g.
15 Fencing gear
16 Lent a hand
17 Finish superficially
20 Similar
21 Supplement (with "out")
22 Moved about energetically
26 Come to grips
30 Disentangled
31 Smudge on Santa
32 Audio receiver
33 Christie's "The Seven ___ Mystery"
34 Pseudonym of H.H. Munro
35 Garage compartments
36 Get right down to business
39 Oodles
40 Beam
41 Whistles when the police are spotted
43 Roman candle path
44 Chuck wagon fare
45 Slim and trim
46 Have through a gene
48 Ms. Clinton
49 Kettle and Barker
50 Bed end
51 Waste no time with
59 Adds one to three, e.g.
60 Gala event
61 Classic opera
62 Dave Thomas' kid
63 Cold feet
64 Contrary current

DOWN

1 Ember, in the end
2 Orchid necklace
3 Harden
4 Bit for the dog bowl
5 Cheated at hide and seek
6 Pest for a rose
7 Restraining influence
8 Powder container
9 Hoop dunk
10 Diaper bag items
11 Shakespearean fuss
12 Where many surf
13 Commercial blurbs
18 Most robust
19 Awe-inspiring
22 Potato eye
23 Horned creature
24 Steadfast
25 Fights with lances
26 Snatched from dreamland
27 Old World prickly plants
28 Outfit of newborn supplies

Puzzle 11

29 Sounds of hesitation
31 Hindu's sir
34 Walk like a chanticleer
35 Genesis tower
37 Beastly (Var.)
38 Must
39 ___ chi (martial art)
42 Coral, for one
44 Flush with fescue
45 April event
47 Improve text
48 Terra ___
50 Complimentary
51 Kittenish call
52 Hail to Caesar
53 He's a real doll
54 Wide of the mark
55 Actress ___ Dawn Chong
56 "The Karate ___" (1984)
57 Roulette play
58 Wray in "King Kong"

EAT WELL

ACROSS

1 Some lunchtime orders
5 Heath bar flavor
11 Like Simon's couple
14 Uxmal sight
15 Gloomy Milne character
16 Dr. of rap
17 Possible theme of this puzzle
20 Sweet-sounding
21 Generous one's words
22 Make like a masseuse
25 Exam for many a college sr.
26 Dairy product with a strong odor
32 On the bounding main
33 Slip the clutches of
34 Italian Riviera town
37 Epitome of limpness
42 Got under the skin of
44 Super's unit, perhaps
45 Objects in a phrase about daftness
51 Skin cream ingredient, often
52 Extensive in scope
53 Gave voice to
57 Ron Howard fantasy flick of 1988
61 Dress rehearsal for an ocean liner?
64 Disney Store collectible
65 Condition marked by chest pains
66 Nat or Natalie
67 Holds title to
68 Delicate hue
69 Door protrusion

DOWN

1 Molding fastener
2 Remarkable person, object or idea
3 Box for bucks
4 Cinema feature
5 Totter partner
6 National anthem preposition
7 Memo abbr.
8 Centers of attention
9 Part of QED
10 Nightfalls, in verse
11 Hans Christian Andersen's birthplace
12 Shakespeare output
13 Keyboard key
18 It's full of options
19 Skin mark
23 Dating from time immemorial
24 Marina ___ Rey
26 Sols' followers
27 "Rose ___ rose" (Stein)
28 Word with foot or fore
29 Nautical steering device
30 CCLI + CL
31 The Chiffons' "___ So Fine"

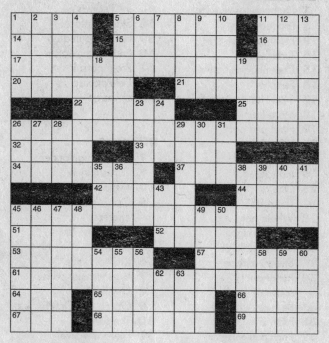

35 Unforgettable time
36 Marie Dressler's Oscar role
38 Unfortunate one's run
39 Troy, New York sch.
40 Enjoyed one's repast
41 Service station combustible
43 Wane
45 Lomb's partner
46 Tennis legend Gibson
47 Doesn't just wreck

48 Go on a quest
49 Diet food type
50 Kind of shake
54 Enjoy, as benefits
55 Dame of theater
56 Let sleeping ___ lie
58 Cowardly one of film
59 Where the Storting sits
60 Coach Ewbank
62 Comic's need
63 Pittsburgh-to-Buffalo dir.

HOME, SWEET HOME

ACROSS

1 Outburst, as of rage
5 Looped cross
9 Front for frost
14 Turkish title
15 Copenhagen native
16 Supply
17 12th Hebrew month
18 More than
19 Fluid pint part
20 HOME
23 Potting need
24 Indisposed
25 One of "The Three B's"
28 Whole note, e.g.
30 Speller's agon
33 "The Bundle of Sticks" author
34 Parking lot souvenir
35 Be rude, in a way
36 HOME
39 Pack contents?
40 "Das Kapital" author
41 Company dodger
42 Film crew's locale
43 Fades away
44 If all goes well
45 Firefighter's need
46 Lot, perhaps
47 HOME
54 Cracks under pressure
55 Ma with a bow
56 Lasso

57 One not seen in "Peanuts"
58 Starting place?
59 Hasn't ponied up
60 Ends of the earth?
61 Prom pursuit
62 Delicate use of words

DOWN

1 Celt or Highlander
2 Citrus variety
3 Avoid unconditionally
4 Oprah and Dr. Phil's offerings
5 Handsome lad of myth
6 Kind of battle
7 Was familiar with
8 "Try this"
9 Oprah and Dr. Phil, e.g.
10 The same
11 Hierarchy level
12 Cursor controllers
13 Copy
21 Pizzazz
22 Numbers game
25 Cowardly flees the scene
26 Even the score again
27 Cash or real estate, e.g.
28 Stadium levels
29 Cameo stone
30 Pickler's need

Puzzle 13

31 A-frame overhangs
32 Critic of Chicago
34 Lacking brightness or color
35 Travel the world
37 Fireplace item
38 Sound start?
43 Is
44 Stage opening
45 Doctor repellent?
46 So far
47 Bring to ruin
48 Heavy hammer
49 Word with googly
50 Word with water or fountain
51 29th of 50
52 Crude bunch?
53 Home tweet home?
54 Patsy

ON THE WING

ACROSS

1 Acts on a preference
5 Marsh plant
10 Put oneself in a hole?
13 Campus club, briefly
14 Lie with limbs spread out
15 Numero ___
16 "Blood and Sand" beast
17 Fez feature
18 ___-Magnon
19 Trite or obvious remark
21 Barely scratched
23 Heat maker
24 Sand bar
25 Like Jerry Lewis characters
26 Norwegian king
30 500 race
31 Polite answer
32 Jay sighted at end of the day
33 Small island
34 Kind of lamp
37 Fidel pal
39 Not just anywhere
40 Mint and sage
44 Store-bought cookie
45 Gemstone
46 The end of ___
47 Funny Jack
49 Like some undergraduate studies
50 Ran out
52 Vacuum tubes
54 Downed
55 Athenian magistrate
57 Drying oven
59 Champagne adjective
60 They're open to discussion
61 Secondhand
62 Too bad!
63 Hit bottom?
64 Hardy heroine

DOWN

1 "___, in the stilly night . . ."
2 Like some legal work
3 Drags one's feet
4 Informers
5 Two-inch nail
6 Gaelic
7 "___ Kapital"
8 Hollywood's Verdon
9 Upper New York Bay island
10 With 53-Down, children's game
11 Caught short
12 Sizable, as an amount
14 Follow a recipe directive
20 Part of MGM
22 Displayed cowardice
23 It's been described as loony

26 Mary-Kate or Ashley
27 Having doubts
28 Building wing
29 Opposition
35 Caught you!
36 Cugat partner
37 Originates
38 Nag, nag, nag
41 Set free
42 Some band instruments
43 Espied

44 Russian province
48 Irish poet
49 Wrestling successes
51 Word with rain or tear
52 Companion of thick
53 See 10-Down
56 Bean counter, for short
58 They often precede kicks, for short

LET'S GO!

ACROSS

1 Wryly amusing
6 Swedish import
10 Abbr. in a real estate ad
14 Like "The Twilight Zone"
15 "___ boy!"
16 Moreno or Hayworth
17 Ward and June's decision?
20 "Monty Python" star
21 With 53-Across, a Beatles song
22 More than required
23 Word with blood or dog
24 Start with school
25 Used "th" in place of "s"
29 Do home work?
34 "___ nous" (confidentially)
35 Brewer's kiln
36 Opposite of stet
37 Lose one's cool
40 It may be tall
41 Aft
42 Heathen
43 They may travel by butterfly
45 Balance sheet item
46 Brian of rock
47 Ring cheer
48 Bogart's role in Casablanca
52 Caesar's welcome
53 See 21-Across

57 Use up all the alibis
60 "That makes ___ of sense"
61 Neighbor of Turkmenistan
62 Dear, as a price
63 Sandwich staple
64 Pullman and passenger, for two
65 Type of bear

DOWN

1 Bagel source, often
2 Bassoon part
3 Verbalized
4 "___, from New York . . ."
5 "Mo' Better Blues" director Spike
6 Full and satisfied
7 Member of a bar assoc.
8 Start of a Vol. 1 heading
9 Yankee legend
10 Bric-a-___
11 Low-class joint
12 66 and others
13 Utopia Plains setting
18 "If ___ a Hammer"
19 Farrow and Gardner, in Sinatra's life
23 "Where's the ___?"
24 Tough question
25 Some turns
26 Nonblood relative
27 Record groove cutters
28 Introduction

29 Punch-line payoff
30 Best and Ferber
31 Marsh plant
32 ___ ease (uncomfortable)
33 High schoolers
35 Alamogordo's county
38 Frantic
39 Church section
44 Computer selection screen
45 Author Haley

47 Many operate on gas
48 Obnoxious young'un
49 Pip
50 Many a lit. author
51 Jot
52 Not nearby
53 Burlap ingredient
54 Secondhand
55 Exploit
56 Catch sight of
58 Man-mouse filler
59 Chicago clock setting

HOW'S THE WEATHER?

ACROSS

1 "Circle" or "final" start
5 Model's makeup?
10 Blow one's lines
14 Barbershop request
15 Long nerve fibers
16 Easy gait
17 Grapefruit hybrid
18 Poker table request
19 "___ out?" (dealer's query)
20 Zeus' weapon
23 Has a bug
24 Call at home
25 Big-ticket
28 ___ monde (society)
30 Word with Wednesday or can
33 Shaw of swing
34 Word with buster or land
35 Word with bump or jump
36 Sensationalism
39 Epitome of craziness
40 Chuckholes
41 Nymph of myth
42 It's sometimes bitter
43 "Are not!" retort
44 Acquiesce
45 Samuel's judge
46 1944 battle site
47 Classic musical
55 "You're making ___ mistake!"
56 "O come let us ___ Him"
57 Prohibited activity
58 Two pounds, plus
59 Old fare on the air
60 Son of Seth
61 Nod neighbor
62 "___ Mia!" (ABBA musical)
63 Glass maven Lalique

DOWN

1 Proof you were at the big game
2 Cogito ___ sum
3 Factory on a stream
4 Not genuine
5 One who orders "the usual," maybe
6 1½ rotation jumps
7 Centers of activity
8 Cozy
9 Like
10 Lighter igniter
11 WKRP's Jennifer
12 Abreast of
13 Baffin Bay sight
21 Snookered
22 1922 Howard Carter discovery
25 Couch potato's lifeline
26 Sweater synthetic
27 Offered one's seat
28 Was given no alternative

Puzzle 16

29 Wee workers
30 Actress MacDowell
31 Place
32 Bunch of huns
34 Hump-shouldered beasts
35 Place for the trapped
37 How lovers stroll
38 Cry of surrender
43 Islam's fourth caliph
44 Parthenon goddess
45 Goad

46 Play a Stratocaster
47 Japanese quaff
48 Footnote abbr.
49 "Cleopatra" backdrop
50 Abstraction
51 Vera's TV husband
52 Top-of-the-line
53 Words after sit or look
54 Rudolph's prominent feature

GET OUT!

ACROSS

1 Pitt of "Kalifornia"
5 Raccoon relative
10 Get naked
14 Olin in "Romeo Is Bleeding"
15 For the birds?
16 Perfect tense word
17 An aura, of sorts
18 Hums like an engine
19 Great place for Chinese or Russian cuisine
20 "Get a grip!"
23 Change-machine insert
24 Tell it like it isn't
25 Jumpy
29 College plaza
31 Bake sale group, perhaps
34 Gumption
35 Crow's-nest locale
36 Club in a bag
37 Feature of many DVDs
40 Rodgers' songwriting collaborator
41 "Holy moley!"
42 Flows like lava
43 Santa ___ winds
44 Between the baselines
45 Most likely to accomplish
46 Oft-heard boot camp word
47 The whole enchilada
48 Dispose of spam?
57 Victor's cry
58 It comes from the heart
59 It's worth about a dollar
60 Cincinnati nine
61 Yarn measure
62 Stick with a stiletto
63 December purchase
64 Sing "nyah-nyah" to
65 Fine-tune

DOWN

1 Solid voters?
2 Go back to square one on
3 Mysterious byline, for short
4 Board sticker
5 Scarface Al
6 Seed-to-be
7 Well-ventilated
8 Poi-making tuber
9 Install fiberglass, perhaps
10 The terrible twos, e.g.
11 Lessen the load
12 Good competitor?
13 Faller in the fall
21 Moore in "Moonraker"
22 Do away with
25 Nebraska city
26 Fireballer Ryan

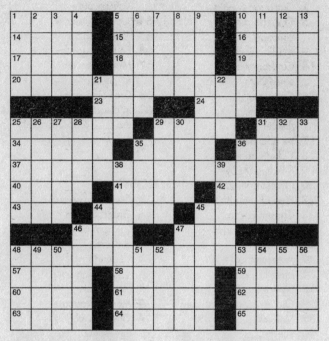

27 More than required
28 Practice girth control
29 Oil emirate
30 Took for a ride
31 Hold dear
32 Firms muscles
33 Apprehensive feeling
35 Wise guys
36 Pop deity
38 Phoenicia locale
39 Type of gas
44 It can be pitched

45 Basic hydrocarbon
46 Touch or taste
47 Those opposed
48 Tabloid gossip
49 Water pitcher
50 Mother of mine?
51 It may be practical
52 Chemical compound
53 Screen material
54 Mercury or Saturn
55 Qom home
56 Ring location?

THE TIME IS NOW

ACROSS

1 Catch forty winks
5 Overcharging concern?
9 Muslim teachers
14 Cut from the same cloth
15 Consumer
16 Old movie theater name
17 Be offended by
18 College sports gp.
19 Mindlessly silly
20 Of lesser importance
22 Fred of Limp Bizkit
23 Christmas carol
24 Leave it, editorially
26 Prohibit
29 Authentic
31 Breakfast order
35 Nebraska city
37 Old Soviet news agency
39 "Miracle ___" (1989)
40 Puerto ___
41 Jerk's creations?
42 Opera solo
43 Stocking shade
44 Choice, for short
45 Flying pests
46 Bogart film "High ___"
48 "Nautilus" captain
50 "Dick and Jane" verb
51 Actress Lollobrigida
53 Swarm
55 Chew out
58 Castles in the air
63 Like some Vatican bulls
64 Japanese people
65 "Dagnabbit"
66 Be the life of the party
67 March fifteenth, to Caesar
68 Crowning point
69 In disarray
70 Pro ___ (proportionate)
71 Moistened clay

DOWN

1 Glen Canyon and Grand Coulee
2 "Grapes of Wrath" character
3 Coating metal
4 "___ a high note"
5 Hogan role
6 Moving staircase
7 One of a storied threesome
8 Cafeteria items
9 Word in footnotes
10 Revolutionary War figure
11 Slightly cracked
12 Certain weekdays (Abbr.)
13 Edible fat
21 Mrs. Nick Charles
25 Play horseshoes
26 Drills a hole
27 Latin friends
28 Mother-of-pearl

30 Heavily burdened
32 Turkish money units
33 Social crème de la crème
34 Add body to hair
36 Primitive timepiece
38 Trapeze artist's security
41 Bridge
45 Word with movie or party
47 "Black Hawk Down" director Scott

49 Snake-haired woman of myth
52 Noted fighter of oil fires
54 Olympic quest
55 Junk mail online
56 "And it ___ to pass . . ."
57 Major musical composition
59 Verdi opera
60 With the bow, in music
61 "I Remember ___"
62 Cherry part

YOU'LL FIND ME INSIDE

ACROSS

1 Eight-track, e.g.
5 Rodeo necessity
10 Lloyd Webber musical role
13 "Fear City" director Ferrara
14 Herr Schindler
15 Not yet up
16 Cornea irritant
17 Aka follower
18 Rosary piece
19 "Keep Out!" follower
22 Nongrammatical case
23 Acrobat catcher
24 Green of "Greg the Bunny"
25 Music genre
28 Bloom of the fall
32 Unit of time
34 Glossed-over place, sometimes
36 Maven
37 He or she
43 Fertility clinic needs
44 Pharmaceutical giant Lilly
45 ". . . there remained not ___." (Ex. 8:31)
46 On edge
49 Net judge's cry
51 Male turkeys
54 Trains on high
56 Virginia Dare's colony
59 Slips and such
64 Spike to shuck

65 Moliere's forte
66 Pedal appendages
67 Pennsylvania city
68 DeGeneres sitcom
69 Italian wine-producing region
70 Block
71 Tiresias and Nostradamus, e.g.
72 ___ majeste

DOWN

1 Gulf city in the Sunshine State
2 Calls off, as a mission
3 Garment size
4 Promotes
5 Reluctant
6 Numb, as a foot
7 Opt to omit
8 River from the Vosges Mountains
9 Mork's supervisor
10 Radio-active driver
11 Qualifying race
12 Oceanic whirlpool
15 Aids in dirty deeds
20 Cause for a blessing
21 Brain size
26 Stan's chum
27 Die spot
29 Chinese "way"
30 Former French coin
31 Half a cartoon couple
33 Compass hdg.

Puzzle 19

35 ___ forma
37 Flower holder
38 Holiday precursor
39 Took off
40 Nothing alternative
41 Ready to use
42 Concerning newborns
47 River of Paris
48 "A Nightmare on ___ Street"
50 Inquiry for a lost package

52 Bummed out
53 Kilters, in poker
55 Items with dials
57 Kicks off
58 Dinsmore of children's books
59 One way to serve coffee
60 Wife in "A Doll's House"
61 It's on your car
62 Fisherman's offering?
63 Perry's creator

"YOU LOOKING AT ME?"

ACROSS

1 "Star Trek II: The ___ of Khan"
6 Go well together
10 "Fernando" singers
14 "Green Acres" character
15 Mixed bag
16 Layer of ore
17 Mixed it up
20 Grant opponent
21 "Mockingbird" singer Foxx
22 Nymphs of Greek myth
23 Made waves?
25 Price fixer
27 From the top
29 Packing material
33 Mixed it up
37 ___ Beta Kappa
38 Gathering dust
39 Infamous Ugandan Amin
40 Big name
41 Barkeep of "The Simpsons"
42 Mixed it up
46 Affirm
48 Sort of sword
49 Beau and Jeff's dad
51 Foil
55 Swamp
58 Currency transaction fee
60 Not the silence of the lambs?
61 Mixed it up
64 First name in diarists
65 Popular cookie since 1912
66 Gentleman's gentleman
67 Stages of a journey
68 Handful of straw
69 Without exception

DOWN

1 Impudent youngster
2 Hindu noblewoman
3 It makes you hot
4 4:00 refreshment, perhaps
5 Sanitary measures
6 Ways and means
7 "My Fair Lady" lady
8 Commandment violation
9 Sinatra's hometown
10 In the wake of
11 Old videotape format
12 Tread-bare
13 City on the Skunk River
18 Put the kibosh on
19 Parts of a house
24 Mass-produce
26 New soft drink of 1961
28 Element of Dr. Seuss' work
30 Capable of
31 Grow genial
32 Jagger and McCartney, e.g.
33 Flaccid

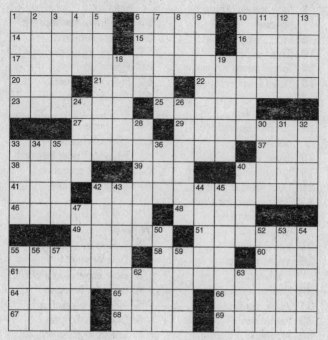

34 Polecat's trademark
35 Marc Antony's love, familiarly
36 Dedicatory verse
40 Seattle ___, the Triple Crown winner
42 Rostropovich's instrument
43 Henceforth
44 Retinal nerve
45 Serve well
47 Lucky breaks

50 NASCAR's Jarrett and Earnhardt Jr.
52 White poplar tree
53 Harder to come by
54 Mouth-watering
55 Inclusive abbr.
56 Love points
57 Saucer-shaped instrument
59 Mawkishness
62 "Exodus" hero
63 Dallas cager, for short

TEMPORARY FIX

ACROSS

1 "___ the wild blue yonder"
5 In ___ way
10 Cpls.' superiors
14 Tango teams
15 "Civil Disobedience," e.g.
16 Trapped like ___
17 "Daniel Boone" actor Ed
18 Type of sofa
19 Knight time?
20 Duct tape, at times
23 Bout ender, for short
24 Shelter for feral animals
25 Individualist
26 Word linking get-here
28 Prefix meaning "gas"
31 ADA member
32 Icy hazard
33 Hopeful
36 Like a Bigfoot sighting, at best
41 Toy dog breed
42 It has eight phases
43 Latin lover's verb
46 Mail-order music name
47 Manhattan Project physicist
48 Superior grade of black tea
50 Teen's collection

52 Bill's "excellent" sidekick
53 Silly idea, perhaps
58 Gray's subj.
59 Burger layer, perhaps
60 Churn up
62 Field of business
63 Author Hector Hugh ___
64 ___ mater
65 "The Owl and the Pussycat" poet Edward
66 Fragrant compound
67 Legal instrument

DOWN

1 Lupino in "Moontide"
2 Dunderhead
3 How some slug it out
4 Bone, in Bologna
5 Inflation protection
6 Like Miss Saigon
7 Letters to answer?
8 Sir's counterpart
9 New Year's Eve word
10 Permission
11 Punish, in a way
12 Prepared for feathering
13 Bull market necessities?
21 Machine that fits in one's hand, briefly
22 It eliminates suspects
23 Fashionable Brit
27 Move in large numbers

28 Stained glass figure, perhaps
29 Some MIT grads
30 Breathing sound
33 Droop in the sun
34 Amount to be raised?
35 Noted plus-size model
37 George of "Star Trek"
38 Cabin feature
39 Erstwhile
40 Geraint's beloved

43 Horrify
44 Bad guy
45 Figure skater Baiul
47 Seminoles' sch.
49 Blender brand
50 Laundry, e.g.
51 Fund contributor
54 Alaskan seaport
55 Wildebeests
56 Shade
57 Gown wearer
61 Whippersnapper

STRIKE UP THE BAND

ACROSS

1 Piglet's mom
4 Milan's La ___
9 Charming woman
14 Rapa ___ (Easter Island)
15 Weighty books
16 Time partner
17 SST's once crossed it (Abbr.)
18 Bakers, really
19 Intimidated
20 Dated "Darn!"
23 Hidden
24 Big Ten sch.
25 Disencumber
28 Child's play
30 Fried Japanese dish
33 Skirt shape
36 Catch
38 Musical Copland
39 Change of heart?
43 Some waves
44 "Scram!"
45 Choice word
46 Less lenient
49 Source of a blast?
51 It adds 10 to 8?
52 Caribbean liquor
54 Reciprocal
58 Symbol of abundance
61 Fabled fabulist
64 Symbol of strength
65 Start of a Thomas Hardy title
66 Regular writing
67 Spanish diacritic
68 Blind rage
69 Not leftover
70 Quite a bit
71 McCourt title

DOWN

1 Fly in the ointment
2 ___ the open
3 Uninhabited regions
4 Swiped
5 Formal agreement
6 "My Cup Runneth Over" singer
7 Slow, in music
8 Lend a hand
9 Forth partner
10 Some may be gigantic in Hollywood
11 Order partner
12 Cypress Point placement
13 Word with tight or loose
21 Hopelessness
22 Word with ball or card
25 Bucolic
26 Removes clotheslines?
27 Divine poet?
29 What golfers try to break
31 Where you may be given some latitude?
32 Color range

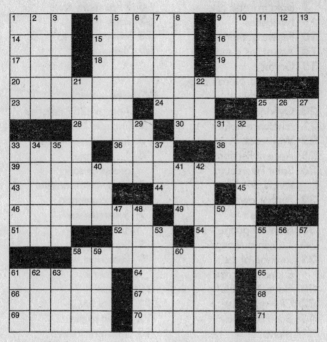

33 Word with
saw or sea
34 Wax eloquent
35 Dandy poet?
37 Do a supermarket job
40 Alternative to
smoking?
41 Tuck partner
42 Bull rush?
47 Blow it
48 Seeks solace from
50 Dour

53 Recurring theme
55 Ill-suited
56 "Dig Dug" maker
57 Ancient instruments
58 It may wind up
on the side of a house
59 Sesame starter
60 Sensed
61 King Kong,
for one
62 Distinctive time
63 Lush

THE WHOLE SHEBANG

ACROSS

1 Data transfer rate
5 Nourishes
10 Festive gathering
14 Adjust, as a motor
15 Garret
16 Nick and Nora's dog
17 In custody
20 Overindulges
21 Tchotchke holder
22 Waistcoat
25 Ancient Persians
26 Saint Petersburg neighbor
30 Further away, in a way
33 Local language
34 "___ in a Manger"
35 Jemison of the Endeavour crew
38 Flaunt the SEC
42 CPR specialist
43 San Pablo Bay island
44 Yankee skipper
45 Fragments
47 Boleyn and Hathaway
48 WWII beachhead
51 Sportscast tidbit
53 Dance or music program
56 Underlings
60 Fun standard, traditionally
64 Leif's father

65 Gloomy
66 It has many slots
67 Pops
68 With regard to
69 Yemen port

DOWN

1 Approx. 252 calories
2 Fritzi, to Nancy
3 Take down, as hair
4 "___ Purple," group or song
5 Many a test answer
6 Ike's command
7 Substitute for the unlisted
8 Bank check?
9 Improvise with numbers?
10 Harass
11 Part of FAQ
12 Cubic meter
13 19th president
18 Bring up to snuff
19 Anthroponym
23 Having only magnitude, but no direction
24 Facing
26 Proverbial healer
27 Famous evictee
28 Excellent condition
29 Hawaiian dish
31 Most current
32 Batiking need

35 "September ___" (Diamond)
36 For some, it could be a lot
37 Achieves with difficulty (With "out")
39 Actress Thurman
40 Borough island
41 32,000 ounces
45 Avoids work
46 Loathing
48 Formed into a circle
49 Actress/comedian Anne
50 Unpleasantly pungent
52 Nautical direction
54 Portrayer of Pierce
55 Desolate
57 Green pod
58 Have to have
59 "Auld Lang ___"
61 Honorarium
62 Irish Sea isle
63 Gun's offspring?

I'M NOT QUITE SURE

ACROSS

1 Curly Howard's replacement
6 Russian pancake
11 Spicy
14 "Mangia!"
15 Angry, and then some
16 Vladimir Nabokov novel
17 Conjecture
19 Spare part
20 Type of coach (Abbr.)
21 Cinco minus cuatro
22 Rise and shine!
24 Brownish-red chalcedony
26 Tight situation
27 State positively
30 Name in a Harold Robbins title
31 With 44-Across, conjecture
33 Persuade
37 Reproductive cells
38 Solid ground
41 Lead-in for Branco or Bravo
42 Dispense
44 See 31-Across
46 Vegetates
49 Slip away, as time
50 Publisher's payment
53 Cosby TV series
54 Tristan's secret love
55 It does a bang-up job
56 Man of Steel's accessory

60 Put down
61 Attempt
64 It may need massaging
65 From the East
66 Joe Louis, for one
67 Referendum choice
68 Aussie tennis star Fraser
69 Tropical nut or palm

DOWN

1 Big name in home video games
2 Herr's home
3 Summers on the Seine
4 Words with "TV" in an old NBC slogan
5 Second letter addendum
6 Hunter's hiding place
7 Wheels for wheels
8 ___ Toguri (Tokyo Rose)
9 Dummy
10 Standards of perfection
11 Concubine center
12 Ill will
13 St. Pete neighbor
18 Chelonian reptile
23 Low islands
25 Graceful steed
26 Stop on a line
27 Molecular component
28 Create interest?
29 Game with 32 cards

Puzzle 24

30 Livestock abodes
32 Uplift morally
34 Finish a take
35 A show of vanity
36 Couple for a brace
39 Coffers
40 Seaweed
43 Airline to Tel Aviv
45 Modern workplace perk
47 River of song
48 Private instruction?

50 NBA coach Pat
51 Inedible orange
52 Toys that go around the world
53 Absurd
55 Pond-dwelling duck
57 Watch for the cops, maybe
58 Glazier's cutting
59 Inclusive abbr.
62 Hyundai competitor
63 Check for drinks

HOLD IT RIGHT THERE!

ACROSS

1 Toast comparative
5 Dust busters?
10 Sellers' market?
14 Fancy needle case
15 Brains, for sure
16 Jiggs' daughter
17 Deutschland divider, once
19 Type of wire
20 Castrogiovanni, today
21 Chemical salts
23 Moroccan's capital
26 Turkey mo.
28 Oka River city
29 Words to the wise
31 Be a pain
33 Bull foe
34 Exasperates
35 Blue
38 Turns gold into lead, e.g.
39 "___ porridge hot . . ."
41 "___ added expense"
42 Variety of whale
43 Kind of film
44 Put in the pen
46 Go by
48 Reduce to rag condition
49 Hammer's target, sometimes
50 Real attachment
52 They come a-courting?

53 Storied invader
55 Nora's terrier
57 "Makes sense!"
58 Boundary one can cross
63 Some disinformation
64 Wipe the slate clean
65 Cut of veal
66 It's absolutely not right!
67 Tear repairer
68 Ho-ho-ho time

DOWN

1 Part of a baseball mitt
2 Filled the bill?
3 Capek's notable play
4 Expense account factors
5 "Buddenbrooks" author
6 Nile-regulating dam
7 "It ___ far, far better thing . . ."
8 Comes through
9 Manche dept. capital
10 Plenary
11 Texas or Vermont, e.g.
12 Tempestuous spirit?
13 Hound sounds
18 Act or play start
22 Pointillist's points
23 Motel posting
24 Be wild about

25 Offshore coral ridge
27 Pain killers
30 Use a sponge or biscuit
32 Shooting sport
36 It must be managed
37 Type A types
40 Chez Hamlet
41 In fact
43 Muslim judge
45 Far from nice
47 Gossip (with "the")

49 Count on the 88s
51 Parson's place
53 Paper producer
54 Good opening pair
56 Hoop ending
59 Car makers' grp.
60 Debtor's paper
61 Zippo
62 Chemical suffix

THIRSTY?

ACROSS

1 Backless footgear
5 Word after 17-, 38-, and 59-Across and 11- and 34-Down
10 Coal carrier
14 Play to ___ (deadlock)
15 Vacuous
16 "Now then, where ___?"
17 Form of liquor smuggling
19 October birthstone
20 Distinguishing feature
21 "Clue" piece
23 Clothes lines?
26 Take ___ off (sit down)
27 Conceal from danger
29 Special talents
32 Jocularity
35 Meadowland
36 Transmitting
37 Infant fare
38 Naval veteran
40 Dull daily routing
41 Show with clarity
43 File suit against
44 Teachers' favorites
45 "The Balcony" playwright
46 You, at this very moment
48 Informed
50 Go awry
54 Steakhouse order
57 Per ___ (yearly)
58 Prefix meaning "bone"
59 Wintertime affliction
62 Letters on some planes
63 Dobie Gillis' buddy
64 Ultimatum's ultimate word, usually
65 Retained
66 Biblical matriarch
67 Penn with an Oscar

DOWN

1 Cuban patriot José
2 Auto maneuver
3 Succotash, in part
4 Least explainable
5 Best the rest
6 ___ Arbor, Michigan
7 Follow furtively
8 Group of nine
9 Majestic
10 Poker holding, perhaps
11 In quick succession
12 Letters of haste
13 Eight furlongs
18 Zion National Park location
22 Give less than 100 percent
24 Choreographer Agnes de ___
25 Tournament ranking
28 Cowboy's apparatus
30 Fastening item
31 Pepper and Preston (Abbr.)

32 Computer image
file format

33 Roof overhang

34 Band in a 1984
film parody

36 Pain relief brand

38 Group of eight

39 New Year's word

42 1960s political movement

44 Charles, William
and Harry

46 Spanish woman's title

47 "The Blackboard Jungle"
novelist Hunter

49 Neil Diamond's
"Love on the ___"

51 Iguanalike critter

52 Oklahoma city

53 German port city

54 Queeg's creator

55 To be, to Brutus

56 "ER" part

60 Wharton deg.

61 City in Kyrgyzstan

BALANCE IT OUT

ACROSS

1 Bleak and desolate
6 Book reviewer, so to speak
9 Flat-headed fasteners
14 Creator of Nancy and Sluggo
15 Trendy
16 Seat belt restraint
17 Some Halloween handouts
19 "The Republic" author
20 Bad Ems, e.g.
21 Thrash
23 Met singer Pinza
24 Distort
25 Painter's device
27 Musician's advantage, say
30 Cheat on one's diet
31 Sty reply
32 Microbiology gel
34 Lagoon encloser
37 Clay transformation?
38 Bright ray
40 ___ Bravo
41 Plant life
43 Asia and thereabouts
44 Eddie Murphy flick
45 Unduly interested
47 Diatribes
49 More severe
52 Pad
53 "Topaz" novelist
54 Laura's 2004 rival
56 Daisy follower

59 Intelligence-gathering group?
61 Brinks stop, at times
63 Perfect little darling
64 Odds and ends abbreviation
65 "Sea of Love" star Barkin
66 Like some voices
67 Victor at Fredericksburg
68 Ketchup rival

DOWN

1 Slangy instants
2 Running play
3 Russian czarina
4 Disburden
5 It's at your fingertips
6 Toast accompaniment
7 Salon treatment
8 Basilica features
9 Salt meas.
10 Minimally
11 Little Bighorn fighter
12 Joey on "Dawson's Creek"
13 Wild animal trace
18 Dresser
22 MD's assistant
24 Round-bottomed pan
26 Take to the road
27 Skate part

28 Fries alternatives
29 Morocco's capital
31 Lummox
33 Mailing address
35 Pitcher projections
36 "The Thin Man" actress
38 Kimono accessory
39 In jeopardy
42 Destination for Shackleton
44 Entrance requirements, sometimes

46 Thus far
48 Century plants
49 Kind of cannonball
50 Staging ground
51 Insurrectionist
55 Appraise
56 Think (over)
57 Pub quaffs
58 Europe's highest volcano
60 Every bit
62 Menu phrase

DUMBO

ACROSS

1 Ayatollah's language
6 Exploit to the max
10 Showed up
14 Item in a cheek pouch
15 "Mourning Becomes Electra" character
16 Munsters' bat
17 The lowdown
19 "___ Man" (1984)
20 Appomattox signatory
21 It may clean itself
22 Show runners
24 Turndowns
25 "___ Swell" (Rodgers & Hart song)
26 Country estates
29 Tell's weapon
33 PLO members
34 Fuel source
35 Year Marcus Aurelius became emperor
36 Dumb one
37 Spaghetti accompaniment
38 Leo's home
39 In the center of
40 Tessellation unit
41 Typeface imitative of handwriting
42 Silver Spring locale
44 Peddled
45 Like the Gobi
46 Brick oven
47 Candy containing fruit
50 Broker's option
51 Vein contents
54 Dairy case spread
55 Rural resident?
58 It's a stretch
59 Coup d'___
60 Pulls down
61 Word with kit or around
62 Adams and Knotts
63 Kind of pen

DOWN

1 Not make the grade
2 Cause of adolescent anxiety
3 "Oliver Twist" girl
4 Mister, in Meerut
5 Like games in the dome
6 Fashions
7 Driver's selection
8 Backtalk
9 Desk type
10 Big-top performer
11 Ex-Met Tommie
12 Sulk
13 Love god
18 Times for celebrating
23 Cal. units
24 Paul Newman film
25 Hint

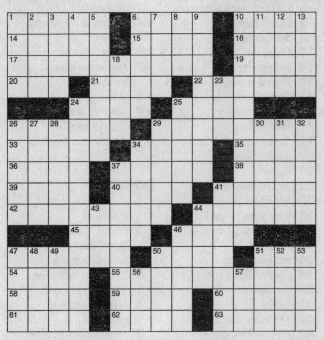

26 Sir's analogue
27 Bakery smell
28 Lowest point
29 "It ___ Happen to You"
30 Empty
31 Zinc ___
32 With a hidden
    microphone
34 Sir Michael
37 Made jump
41 Long-distance
    auto races (Var.)

43 Hula hoop?
44 Over the ___
46 English odist
47 Revolver name
48 Hodgepodge
49 In-basket item
50 Read a bar code
51 Creole veggie
52 Flat fee
53 ". . . or ___!"
56 Oklahoma tribe
57 Cereal grass

NO WAY!

ACROSS

1 Units of work in physics
5 Dutch island in the Caribbean
10 Hoax
14 Nitty-gritty
15 Pinball move
16 Oscar-nominated role for Shirley
17 Deli offering
19 Crazy-sounding bird
20 Ancient bazaar
21 Rational
22 Stomach-turning
23 Impatient (to go)
25 It may be loaded
27 Site of many scrapes
28 Sore
31 HS underlings
34 Pacific island group
36 Succeed
37 Collar
40 Muscular canine
42 "___ will be done"
43 School no-show
45 More loathsome
47 Swinging joint?
48 Hunt for
49 Send out
53 Goldsmith's concern
55 Llama cousin
57 World's most northern desert
59 Shipshape
62 Big name in cosmetics
63 Word with house or shop
64 Abode of a grouchy Muppet
66 Caps
67 Amherst campus, familiarly
68 Wise
69 Song or slug follower
70 Slender maiden
71 Went like a leadfoot

DOWN

1 Commence, as a venture
2 Noted "Death Valley Days" host
3 In large supply
4 O. Henry collection
5 Winner on court
6 Alpha, beta and gamma
7 Major constellation?
8 Outlaw hunter's reward
9 Fossilized resin
10 Computer chip material
11 Working mom's cooker
12 Out of control
13 Umpteen
18 One of the Bobbsey clan
24 Full range
26 Etymologist's interest
29 Gen. wannabe
30 Share and share alike

32 Come again?
33 Hog home
35 Doubleday of baseball myth
36 Bohemian dance
37 Certain degree
38 Shipping magnate Onassis
39 Kids' spacesaver
41 Peter out
44 Con
46 Hold back

48 Amorous
50 Zany
51 Mammoth film of 2002?
52 Made into leather
54 Black Scottish cattle
56 Fall behind
57 "A good walk spoiled" according to Twain
58 Ron Howard role
60 Sea near the Caspian
61 Kitchen meas.
65 Fireplace residue

PERFECT SPECIMENS

ACROSS

1 Pogs and Furbys
5 Rainbow goddess
9 Confound
14 "Hard ___!" (helmsman's cry)
15 Element no. 10
16 At no time
17 Cerebellum section
18 Certain short skirt
19 Playoff setting, sometimes
20 In great shape
23 Pond denizen
24 The go-to guys on staffs
25 Articulates
29 Eviscerate
30 Married Italian woman
31 Spick-and-span
34 Narrow strip of wood
36 Cork source
37 In excellent condition
41 Brain wave record
42 It's good when they meet
43 Church recesses
44 Sarcastic
47 Part of a Morse code letter
48 What tennis balls are packaged in
49 Support in wrongdoing
51 Calendar abbr.

54 In fine fettle
57 Copal or mastic
60 Electricity conductor
61 Approximation
62 Amid
63 Aroma if pleasant, smell if bad?
64 Exclamation of sorrow
65 Ridges of wind blown sand
66 Oculist's piece
67 Ancient musical instrument

DOWN

1 Trumped-up
2 Emotionally detached
3 Broadway opening
4 Scene homophone
5 Still in one piece
6 Recycle
7 Very small amounts
8 Cold-shoulder
9 Similar to another thing
10 Arthurian magician
11 Cousin of St. or Blvd.
12 Buddhist sect
13 Bullpen stat
21 Intimidate
22 Andrew Lloyd Webber musical
26 Denver's Field
27 Obliterate
28 "Land ___ alive!"
29 OJ buy

Puzzle 30

30 Insolence
31 Flimflam
32 Freeloader
33 Enthusiastic
34 Put in harmony
35 "A Shropshire ___"
38 It should set off alarms
39 Country on the island of Hispaniola
40 Choose
45 Process, as sugar
46 Homo sapiens, e.g.

47 Yields
49 Stage whisper, perhaps
50 Title of nobility
51 Strangely
52 Understandable
53 Display poor sportsmanship
55 MP's prey
56 I-XII locale
57 X-ray unit
58 Cassowary kin
59 Jupiter, to Saturn

BODY PARTS

ACROSS

1 Adenoidal
6 Short-winded
11 X-ray cousin
14 "Be-Bop-___" (Gene Vincent hit)
15 Perceived by the ear
16 Auric's creator
17 Strenuous exertion
19 Set afire
20 Carreras, for one
21 Tax type
23 Car loan initials
25 Kind of cheese
28 Rider's handful
29 Thumb (through)
31 Snoop
34 House & Garden topic
36 Word with chuck or covered
37 Being tested or tried
40 Grammy winner Manchester
44 Ancient Hebrew prophet
46 Dud on wheels
47 Assent without action
52 Like Alex Rodriguez, sometimes
53 Feverish chill
54 Java emanation
56 Bad thing to break
57 "I don't believe my eyes!"
60 Word with basin or wave

62 Fingerlings-to-be
63 Pedestrian shoppers
68 Bard's before
69 Two to one, for one
70 Noted game show announcer
71 Paced the field
72 Time after time
73 Lovers' rendezvous

DOWN

1 Glasgow turn-down
2 One hundred percent
3 Take away
4 Burn balm
5 Some bowling sites
6 Bodega setting, perhaps
7 Quebec street
8 Keogh relative
9 Alleviate
10 Show muscle?
11 Environment
12 Cookie addition, perhaps
13 Denote or connote
18 Word with evening or night
22 Political pals
23 Tough-guy actor Ray
24 Claw alternative
26 Chicago-to-Memphis dir.
27 It's in stitches
30 Emulate Cassandra

32 Get more mature
33 Turn over and over
35 Work up
38 Cause of inflation
39 Hawaiian bubbly?
41 Pip-squeak
42 Couch potato's place
43 With a clean slate
45 Paul McCartney title
47 Hardy partner
48 Pay no heed to
49 Put through a blender

50 T-shirt material
51 Kuwaiti head
55 Rewrite for
Hollywood
58 Voluminous do
59 Lounge around
61 Off in the distance
64 Baseball great Mel
65 Casual Friday
castoff
66 Bouncers read them
67 Barracks bed

ALL AROUND THE HOUSE

ACROSS

1 "Abraham, Martin and John" singer
5 Switch partner
9 Family men
14 Part of a magician's phrase
15 It could be part of a plot
16 Woolly-haired cud chewer
17 Scouts' supervisor
19 Its first is for fools
20 Certain playing marble
21 Roald Dahl book
23 What libraries do
24 Nevada's second largest city
25 Knights-in-training
28 Word with ill, well or mild
32 "Tut-tut!"
33 Purplish colors
35 Fish with a long snout
36 Bestowed titles
37 Sisters' three
38 Until all hours
39 Swell place?
40 Sleep inducers, once
41 "Rag Mop" brothers
42 Arrange with some effort
44 They take the cake
45 Heading for morph

46 Aka H.H. Munro
48 Hard to interpret
51 Place for Earl Grey and light snacks
55 Natural talent
56 Between-classes area
58 Quiz answer, perhaps
59 Construction wood
60 Lamb's "Essays of ___"
61 Knight's mount
62 Goes on and on and . . .
63 Claim innocence

DOWN

1 Some family members
2 "Likely story!"
3 Alençon is its capital
4 How some shall remain
5 Drive home, as a run
6 Yearned
7 Fury
8 Prison stretch
9 Typewriter rollers
10 Skiing style
11 Charades or Pictionary, say
12 Centrally located
13 Hacienda room
18 Shouts at a bullfight
22 "Gunsmoke" star

25 Like yesterday's news
26 Completely unfamiliar
27 Neighborhood event
28 One deep in thought
29 State point-blank
30 Polished-off
31 Kind of rehearsal
33 Sort of shower
34 Arthur ___ Stadium
38 Expended profusely

40 Hung in there
43 Cut into
44 Word of assent
46 Was awful
47 Culex's cousin
48 Switch positions
49 Utter loudly
50 Glimpse from afar
52 Hearty partner
53 Lena of "Havana"
54 Kind of bill
57 Familia member

GET SOME R AND R

ACROSS

1 Guarded get-together
6 Equivalent
10 Bailiwick
14 "Jeopardy!" sign
15 Austen novel made into a movie
16 Time divisions
17 Boot camp arrival
19 Paint remover
20 Like eyes, at a sad movie
21 A malarial fever
22 "Julia" portrayer
26 Restraining rope
28 Ready to sail
29 Bug's antenna
31 Places for oars
32 Form component
33 Water you can walk on
36 Analogous
37 Secures with cables
38 Gulf in the news
39 Modern Clay
40 Kind of cabinet
41 Echo, e.g.
42 Parts of the family
44 Loath
45 Lake Huron port
47 Consecrated
48 Beat a path
49 Eddie of the sportswear chain
51 Justice's garb
52 Where shots are heard

57 Girlfriend in Grenoble
58 Type of history
59 Emollient sources
60 Pixie stick
61 Is mistaken
62 Red-spotted creatures

DOWN

1 Rocky crag
2 Stuff studied in genetics
3 Swerve, as a ship
4 "Hey, mister!"
5 Earth movers?
6 Iceberg to an ocean liner
7 Ratite birds
8 Disembogue
9 Tattle
10 Poke holes in, perhaps
11 Theodore Roosevelt's group
12 Come as a consequence
13 Fall flower
18 Unfriendly
22 Lily type
23 Bubbling on the range
24 Doo-wop hit
25 Tool shed item
26 Adder's column
27 Man in a lodge
29 Penguin perches

30 Post a gain
32 Word with "china" or "spur"
34 Fire starter
35 Ran its course
37 Easily cleaved mineral
38 Father of Fear and Panic
40 Party souvenir
41 Exceeded limits
43 "You don't say!"
44 Toward the sheltered side
45 Horse stall sighting
46 It stimulates a sense
47 Jordan's team
49 100 Ethiopian cents
50 A distant point
52 Caviar, literally
53 Publican's serving
54 Then partner
55 Grasp
56 Back-and-forth curve

VERBIAGE

ACROSS

1 A Leeward Island
6 Gaping hole
11 The highest status
14 Big name in household cleaning
15 Aka Myanmar
16 Dr. J's one-time league
17 Stay in the shade
19 Burns of documentaries
20 Blacken, in a way
21 Atomic energy org.
22 Connecticut collegian
23 Deep cuts
26 Worse than inadequate
28 AAA recommendation
29 Title for Coptic bishops
31 Ebenezer's exclamation
32 Country in the news
34 Van Gogh had one in his later years
35 Grandparents, often
38 Mixed with water
40 Dictionary
41 Shiny cotton fabric
42 ___ Lingus
43 Wine county
44 "Ben-___"
45 Garlic bulb segment
47 Frat party staple
48 Pollyannaish
51 Wedges in firmly (Var.)
53 Friend of Wynken and Blynken
54 Like some vbs.
55 Conversation filler
56 Be in the red
57 Be just what the doctor ordered
62 Acapulco aunt
63 Perfect
64 Where to find clowns
65 Sea delicacy
66 "The First Noel," for one
67 The rain here falls mainly on the plain

DOWN

1 Celebrant's robe
2 "A pocketful of ___ . . ."
3 "Dream Team" letters
4 Make a mess of
5 Tennis player Gibson
6 Good buddy, often
7 "What did you say?"
8 Gladiators' milieus
9 Like Mensa members
10 Car maker of note?
11 Be extraordinary
12 Manuscript marks
13 Stock market crash preceder
18 Many a one-hit wonder, today
23 Components of crosswords
24 Heart chambers
25 Make it official

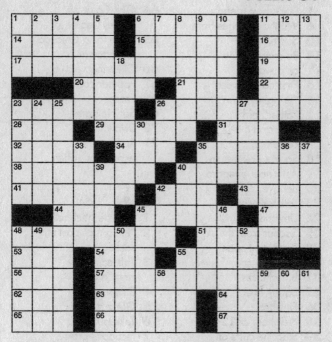

26 Golfer's goal,
at the least

27 Eschew the restaurant

30 Michael Jackson album

33 Waiting line

35 Whirling one

36 Captured at a
64-Across

37 Unexpected obstacles

39 "That's wonderful!"

40 Fifth sign

42 Nothing partner

45 Ringlet-producing gadget

46 Mideast bigwigs

48 Bill called a Benjamin

49 Mr. Mandel

50 Role for Salma

52 Jazz genre

55 "___ cost you!"

58 ___-Tse (Chinese
philosopher)

59 "Rhoda" mom

60 Wahine's gift

61 Contemporary of Bela

LETTER GRADE

ACROSS

1 Doc's best friend
6 Withhold wages from
10 Sacred bird
14 Be overattentive, as a waiter
15 First name in scat
16 "Bringing Up Father" girl
17 ". . . and the ___ of defeat"
18 Sprat's preference
19 Astronaut Shepard
20 Behave
23 Latish lunchtime
24 Unvaried
25 Spoiler from the sky
28 Prominent span of years
31 Bar choices
35 Barley fibers
36 Finished
38 Neighbor of 12-Down
39 Slap the cuffs on
40 Pencil game entries
42 Beach color
43 Bleak, in verse
45 They're cut by dancers
46 Discovery
47 Sketch over
49 Ring around the collar?
50 Swing a scythe
51 Tournament freebies
53 Before of yore
55 Complete a contract

63 Passing sentences?
64 "The Color of Money" game
65 Place for a Chicago touchdown?
66 Glittering vein
67 Popular cookie brand
68 Fracas
69 Satyric stare
70 Swallow flat
71 Rathbone's expression, often

DOWN

1 George Michael's group
2 "Pic-a-nic" basket seeker
3 This company rings a bell
4 Sinews
5 Get a feel for
6 Take-out order?
7 Picador's praise
8 Puts palms together
9 Dorothy's home
10 In a silly manner
11 Font property, sometimes
12 Mideast country
13 Word preceding souci or serif
21 Requisites
22 Squirrel away
25 Short time off to relax?
26 In the know

27 Under cover
29 Sound from Simba
30 Make void
32 Shaw of swing
33 Prince Harry's mom
34 Wall St. "500"
37 You're tense on this
40 Physician's photos
41 Willow for wicker
44 Dispute settler
46 Add ice, as to an old drink

48 It can be concealed
52 Napper's noise
54 Suite things
55 Kewpie
56 Clarinet cousin
57 Surfer's concern
58 The Johns we don't know
59 Congeal
60 Telemarketer's aim
61 December purchase
62 Soothsayer

CARRY THE TORCH

ACROSS
1 Bubble-headed
6 Part of a pigskin?
10 Goulash, e.g.
14 Convex moldings
15 Jai ___
16 Classic sitcom
17 Talking black bird
18 Gunfire sound
19 First name of first American in space
20 Compete at 39-Across
23 CBS drama
26 Vitiate
27 A score
28 "Just a sec"
30 Swank
31 Bit of legalese
32 He sang with Crosby
35 Kind of pollution
39 International event
42 Military nickname
43 A means to an end?
44 Bean counters (Abbr.)
45 Classic TV tosspot
47 Stick like glue
49 Strand
52 Church area
54 Mag. edition
55 2004 site of 39-Across
58 Part of a low poker straight
59 One way to be tickled

60 "Way to go!"
64 Give credit to
65 Tony's cousin
66 Get rid of
67 Responsibilities, so to speak
68 Ball-bearing group?
69 Bear claw alternative

DOWN
1 ___ Perignon (expensive French champagne)
2 It can climb up on campus
3 Simple conclusion?
4 Coal furnace waste
5 Pirate's call
6 Work hard
7 Eyeopener?
8 Quitter's contraction
9 H's position
10 1939 John Wayne classic
11 Falcon's foot
12 Put on a pedestal
13 Full of hot air
21 Kind of pack
22 Hagman's oilman
23 Communicates online
24 "Peter and the Wolf" bird
25 Prefix meaning between
29 Lovers may make them

30 Bar tab
33 Concert gadgets
34 Place for a massage
36 The John F. Kennedy Library architect
37 Mail-order pioneer Richard
38 Twisting turns
40 Reveal
41 Pursue
46 The place to be seen
48 Floored

49 Cigarette lighter
50 Skylit lobbies
51 Scarlett's love
52 Golfer with an "army"
53 Diminutive dogs
56 Pointed remark
57 Dollar competitor
61 Rather good at delivering news?
62 Buckeye school (Abbr.)
63 Harden

THE GREAT DEBATE

ACROSS

1 ___ and all (as is)
6 Draw in
10 Word of hearty concurrence
14 Ready for anything
15 Made cheddar better
16 Sheltered spot
17 Weathercaster's tool
18 Plug in the mouth
19 Delineated
20 Gifted child's performance, perhaps
23 Compass heading
24 On a roll
25 Star of the rotation
28 Tang anagram
31 Tyrannous type
36 Apple or pear
38 Face-to-face exam
40 Alan Ladd classic
41 This could get you a "TV-MA" rating
44 "Uncle!"
45 Grain storage locale
46 Give a hand?
47 Ogles
49 Glaswegian headgear
51 Resort in the Ardennes
52 It has a wet floor
54 NASA thumbs-up
56 Construction superintendent's nightmare

65 Auspicious
66 Wart cause, in folklore
67 Private preceptor
68 Assures, in slang
69 "Not ___ many words"
70 Chopin piece
71 Urbane fellow
72 Dear partner?
73 Compensate

DOWN

1 "Star Trek" speed
2 Apple treatment, once
3 Change the look of
4 Word with "secret" or "school"
5 Kind of bikini
6 Full of frills
7 Sounds of disgust
8 Arm's length
9 Depp role
10 Current choice
11 Oliver Twist's request
12 From now on
13 Ex-speaker's name
21 Salami city
22 1998 headline event in India
25 Doctor repellent?
26 Feldman of "Stand By Me"
27 Get melodramatic
29 Two of all fours
30 Unspoken
32 Tool repository

33 Glass squares
34 Ready for use
35 Current wizard
37 Poacher's needs?
39 "Copacabana" showgirl
42 Play reveille
43 Start of a Donne quote
48 Jelly ingredient
50 More malleable
53 Words before time or another?

55 Fonda-Sutherland film
56 Libertine's opposite
57 Wedding shower?
58 Candid
59 Wisecrack
60 Hombre's dwelling
61 Landfill problem
62 Words with live or give
63 Sonata finale
64 Part of a low straight

EAT UP!

ACROSS

1 4-0 World Series win, e.g.
6 Abraded
10 Airport queue
14 Co-creator of "The Flintstones"
15 Dead Sea region
16 Peace Prize city
17 Yale of Yale University
18 Bunker buster
19 Where esnes slaved
20 Morning eating place
23 GI with stripes
24 Smaller than small
25 One-time protest site
31 Brothers of soul
32 Island-hopper's stop
33 Brewpub feature
36 Can't do without
37 Mushroom stem
38 Ruinous agent
39 Stumble
40 "I ___ Song (In My Heart)" (Gladys Knight)
41 Bridge directions
42 Dapper one's wear
44 Just say yes
47 Biblical lifesaver
48 End-of-the-day noshes
55 Fall into a chair
56 "Waiting for the Robert ___"
57 Dazzling effect
58 Roll-call yell
59 Reporter's quest
60 Fuel-yielding rock
61 Service closer
62 Big top, e.g.
63 Creedal statement

DOWN

1 "The Purple People Eater" singer Wooley
2 A ridge, especially on cloth
3 "Idylls of the King" character
4 Highlighted
5 Corpulent
6 Friday on TV
7 Shark stimulus
8 City on seven hills
9 Fortify, as a town
10 Strongbox
11 Like the yak
12 Smile on
13 Sentimental soul
21 Happy associate
22 Stem-to-stern part
25 Come-on
26 Web surfer
27 Cub or Met, for short
28 Granola-like
29 Being of service
30 Like some stock

33 Tedious undertaking
34 Kick in to a pot
35 Royal pain
37 Feeling
38 It could cause
one to lie down
on the job
40 Huckleberry or Mickey
41 Heartfelt
42 Intensify
43 Bk. after Hebrews
44 Omega's antithesis

45 City of witch hunts
46 Part of some chains
49 Exultation
50 Chopped down
51 Crammer's concern
52 Family group
53 Crinkly cabbage
54 Leave in after all

SHRINK WRAP

ACROSS

1 Economical Halloween costume
6 Gin flavoring
10 ". . . sting like ___"
14 Beauty queen adornment
15 The Piltdown man, e.g.
16 "Agreed!"
17 Suffering from nyctophobia
20 Zero, in soccer
21 Heist haul
22 Maltreat
23 Helvetica, for one
24 Equipped
25 Brings down
28 Bird of Old Rome
29 CBS show set in Las Vegas
32 Not moving
33 Without ___ (daringly)
34 Hemoglobin component
35 Xenophobia
38 Object of desire?
39 Settles with certainty
40 Send to seventh heaven
41 School of tomorrow?
42 Dolt
43 Examine
44 Shed, snake-style
45 Pro ___ (free)
46 One way to be washed

49 Spring bloom
50 Ceiling figure
53 Suffering from zoophobia
56 Home of ancient Irish kings
57 Triumphant cry
58 Pathogens
59 Follow the code
60 Meshworks
61 Explosive trial

DOWN

1 "___ the Man" Musial
2 CD player ancestor
3 Sandwich man?
4 Slice of history
5 Adapt for
6 "Go ahead and ask"
7 Studio site, sometimes
8 Bit in a horse's mouth?
9 Initial bit of evidence
10 Discombobulate
11 Gal's sweetheart
12 They usually listen well
13 Sommer of films
18 Gangland bigwigs
19 Pipe bends
23 Take to the bank?
24 Says with no uncertainty
25 Permanent pen pal?
26 Bridge bid, briefly

27 Intertwine
28 Paid to play
29 Floorboard sound
30 To some degree
31 Map feature
33 Knotted neckwear
34 Home of "Nanook of the North"
36 Worked as a sub
37 Advertising lure
42 Heart
43 Cut of meat

44 Coral reef denizen, perhaps
45 Grain husks
46 Concerning
47 Striker's anathema
48 Fabled napper
49 "___ ain't broke . . ."
50 Supervision
51 Poor box donations
52 "Hey, over here!"
54 Have bills
55 Bumped into

MIDDLE TO REAR

ACROSS

1 "Couldn't have said it better myself"
5 There's no accounting for it
10 Turkish topper
13 Amount spent
14 Greek alphabet starters
16 George's musical brother
17 Nature personified
19 LL Cool J output
20 Zeta-theta connection
21 Courage
22 Cheer for the matador
24 Assemble
26 Owing on one's payments
30 Negligent
32 Clinging part of a climbing plant
33 Start to dominate?
34 Cartridge holder
35 Mortar rounds
36 Bygone
39 Weaselly critters
42 One way to follow a pattern
43 ___ mater (brain membrane)
45 Long, long time
46 Type of reaction
48 Pizza sauce enhancer
50 Respectable
53 Shuffle
55 Has down pat
57 Butting bighorn
58 Molded, frozen dessert
60 By way of
61 Slugging stat
63 A bit too serious
66 Valdez cargo
67 40th president of the U.S.
68 Player's stake
69 "About a ___" (2002 film)
70 Improve, as a text
71 Angler's prize

DOWN

1 Heights of perfection
2 More debatable
3 Elvis' Graceland, e.g.
4 Unspecific degree
5 Poi source
6 French historian de Tocqueville
7 New World colonizer
8 Imperil
9 Gormandize
10 Combat supplies
11 Historical time
12 Laser gun sound effect
15 Like many a sheep
18 Napoleon's realm
23 "___ and the Swan" (Yeats)
25 Guy who cries foul
27 Back out
28 Frost

29 Give me a brake?
31 Star close to Venus?
34 Word with fraternity or hair
36 Olfactory perception
37 Tackle box item
38 Without much cheer
40 Night light
41 Chump
44 Indian tourist site
47 Comaneci accomplishment

49 Museum suit
50 Abase
51 Repeated Catholic prayer
52 Ironic turns
54 Eat more than one's fill
56 Eats more than one's fill
59 Boston or Chicago, e.g.
61 Scottish hero Roy
62 Short life story?
64 Rock singer Bobby
65 Capture a crook

WELL-SUITED

ACROSS

1 Vain claim
6 "Venus de ___"
10 Be a misanthrope
14 Kind of wave
15 Four Corners state
16 Roman love poet
17 Where many are thrown out
20 Part of the eye
21 ___ Aviv
22 Traffic sign
23 Limited number
25 Opposite of "yippee!"
26 Outward flow
29 Yard tool
35 Afternoon social
36 Treats with milk
37 Computerphile
38 Ranch workers
40 Rap physician
41 Bisected
42 Homophone of 41-Across
43 City on the Gulf of Aqaba
45 U.K. lexicon
46 Place to socialize
49 Reuben bread
50 Flu symptom, perhaps
51 Clerical abbreviation
53 Part of LIFO
56 Executive's deg.
58 Cockpit guesses, for short
62 Synthetic pump
65 "So long!"
66 Word with the wiser
67 "Whether she work in land ___" (Emerson)
68 Tall tale
69 Crystal consulter
70 Piece in Harper's

DOWN

1 Hindi courtesy title
2 Any of several Norse royals
3 Concha, in architecture
4 Bound collection
5 Keyboard key
6 Lazy animal?
7 Work with "do" or "cost you"
8 Stripling
9 Orville or Wilbur Wright, e.g.
10 Rustic
11 Confess openly
12 Ginger portrayer ("Gilligan's Island")
13 Water whirl
18 Not just feuding
19 Symbols of industry
24 They can be inflated or boosted
25 Turn over, as property
26 Body of values
27 Game of chance
28 African language group
30 Late plane ride
31 Corinthian's cousin

32 Fur trader John Jacob
33 Decimal preceder?
34 Wear away
39 Act of philanthropy
41 "What'll ___?"
(bartender's question)
44 Perceived by the ear
47 End-of-week cry
48 Quarrels
52 Alters a schooner's
direction
53 Like a bertha collar

54 Opera highlight
55 Betelgeuse or Vega
56 Selfish one's exclamation
57 1934 heavyweight
champ Max
59 Ex-Soviet news agency
60 Vicinity
61 Reprieve from
the governor
63 Two-time 1500-meter
Olympic gold medalist
64 Bladed pole

MY APOLOGIES

ACROSS

1 "Back in Black" band
5 Sell for
10 Hat part
14 "Gone With the Wind" mansion
15 Sine, for one
16 Cryptic character
17 "The ___ lama, he's a priest" (Nash)
18 Regarding
19 Man, but not woman
20 Part of an apology
23 Heels
24 Parking place
25 Religious residence
28 Not busy
30 Is for many?
33 Pint part
34 "This weighs ___!"
35 Calla lily's family
36 Part of an apology
39 Fresh-mouthed
40 Penetrating look?
41 Imposing residence
42 It's on display
43 Ruined
44 Union matter
45 Word with "juris" or "generis"
46 Seaweed, e.g.
47 Part of an apology
54 Stew or miscellany
55 Figure of speech
56 Riding whip
58 First name in fragrance
59 Bait
60 Juno, to the Greeks
61 Hoard
62 Chips in chips
63 Pitcher that can't pitch

DOWN

1 Words before Z
2 "___ quote you on that?"
3 Harriet Beecher Stowe book
4 Gingham dog combatant
5 St. Bernard's supply
6 Blows off steam
7 Article
8 Number of Muses
9 Behaved
10 Ekland of film
11 Bum's ___ (ejection)
12 "To Live and Die ___"
13 Convene
21 Tempts fate
22 "Stat!"
25 Family man
26 Straightedge
27 Like neon
28 Mink kin
29 Australasian parrot
30 Sports complex

31 It may be spread
32 Nail smoother
34 It's also known as a natural
35 Himalayan danger
37 Initial piece of evidence
38 Publicist's concern
43 Apt name for a lawyer
44 Attacks a la "Ghostbusters"

45 Hawk's descent
46 "___ by any other name . . ."
47 Tilt one's head
48 Skin-cream additive
49 "Good work!"
50 Fall place?
51 Edict
52 Took a card
53 Feeling miffed
57 It's for the course

UNDERGROUND OR UNDERCOVER

ACROSS

1 Beatlesque hairstyles
5 Kind of radio
9 Parts of Scottish accents
14 "___ Brockovich"
15 Water or land sport
16 Sci-fi writer Asimov
17 Brahms' "___ Rhapsody"
18 Dropped leaflets, perhaps
20 See 58-Down
22 Singapore sling ingredient
23 Center or cure beginning
24 Put down
25 Confirmation phrase
27 Pre-Lenin Russian ruler
29 Revolving firework
31 K-Mart, for one
33 Epistles writer
34 Sanyo competitor
38 See 58-Down
41 Eye problem
42 Some deer
43 Striped critter
44 ". . . with ___ in sight"
46 Electrical safeguard
47 Big name in small planes
50 ___ Lingus
51 USSR successor
54 Tokyo tie
55 See 58-Down
59 Famed Italian educator
61 Earthenware pot
62 Bar in Fort Knox
63 Terrible czar
64 Plumbing problem
65 Some Duma votes
66 Word before time and place
67 Salinger character

DOWN

1 Gettysburg figure
2 Fourth deck of a ship
3 Type of gland
4 Arrogant and annoying person
5 Show up
6 Snakelike fish
7 Beat badly
8 Brood about
9 Foot part
10 Olympic dream team
11 Shortstop's asset
12 Forearm bones
13 Hardly any
19 Saintly founder of scholasticism
21 Grassy plain
26 Holds responsible
28 Warning sounds
29 Dwindled
30 Kisses companions
31 The "eye" in broadcasting

32 Castaway's dwelling
33 Subatomic particle
35 Silly individuals
36 Tolstoy title start
37 Chicken-king connector
39 Creates, as havoc
40 Light blue
45 Beginnings
46 Catlike
47 Sam & Dave's "Hold On! I'm ___"
48 Wood from India and Sri Lanka
49 Burn off feathers or hair
50 James ___ Garfield
52 Koran religion
53 Execute an unwritten agreement, in a way
56 Egyptian fertility goddess
57 Astral flareup
58 20-, 38-, or 55-Across
60 Rug rat

WHERE'S DAD?

ACROSS

1 Duplicate, for short
6 Accomplishment
10 "She's a Lady" songwriter
14 Louis L'___, writer of Westerns
15 "D'amor sull'ali rosee," e.g.
16 Clod
17 Satisfy the skeptics
20 A swill place
21 Procures
22 Bean variety
23 Exquisite
24 Palm reader's words
25 Rules of behavior
29 Child's amt.?
32 Two-time MVP quarterback
33 Site of some monkey business
34 Wiesbaden wife
35 Wizard's gift to the lion
36 One of the Berenstains
37 Remorse
38 Social event for Scarlett
39 Pledge
40 Most achy
41 "Bravo!"
42 Continuously
44 Storage containers
45 "Calm down"
46 Nook
49 Cross-country necessity?
50 Fitness promoter
53 Really boring
56 "Shoot!"
57 Word with booster or bucket
58 Sleep disrupter
59 Closes the gap, in a way
60 With competence
61 Sox foes

DOWN

1 Dosimeters measure them
2 Give off, as light
3 Nosegay
4 Ingredient of black bottom pie
5 Nonconformist
6 Went hungry
7 Distinctive times
8 Feel rotten
9 Converses with
10 Living quarters
11 Common word?
12 Laker named for a steak
13 Rather pretentious
18 Transmits
19 Loses energy, as a battery
23 Like some consequences
24 Wise to
25 Animated pachyderm
26 "Tough Guys Don't Dance" star Ryan
27 Move furtively

28 Longtime Boston conductor
29 Sampled
30 Ketchup rival
31 It'll fill in the cracks
34 Bearlike, in a way
36 Pleasures
37 Vanishes
39 Oscar-winning portrayer of Julia
40 Squirrel away
42 Super soprano

43 Full of spunk
44 Emblems on the Chargers' helmets
46 Sticks in
47 Entice
48 Lobster delicacy
49 Druggist's container
50 The other Berenstain
51 Employment bonus
52 Ordnance
54 Society girl, briefly
55 ___ mode

WHICHEVER

ACROSS

1 Avian food holder
5 Lighter igniter
10 Meal fit for a pig
14 "O patria mia" singer
15 Kind of feedback
16 Overcome trials
17 Delight, as a comedy club crowd
18 Polar ship or tension reliever
20 "Desire Under the ___"
21 Fleur-de-___
22 Hardly straight
23 Readied the bow
25 Niagara Falls condition
27 Alit
29 It makes food seem good or bad
33 One with seniority
34 Icy shower
35 Pickable
36 Homophone for eight
37 Berry with Oscar
38 Restorative resort
39 Except
41 Some are behind glasses
42 None of the above
44 Supporting towers for a bridge
46 Animal trails
47 Outdoors
48 Gym iteration
49 Perpendicular to the keel
52 Mythical bird of prey
53 Ivan or Nicholas
56 Dairy product or Dale Evans' mount
59 Unbleached linen color
60 Like a certain eagle, wolf or ranger
61 Long and narrow strip of water
62 Type of forest
63 Nestling hawk
64 Agassi of tennis
65 Minor dispute

DOWN

1 Grammatical category
2 Wee brook
3 Famous couple or North American orchid
4 Inn for Longfellow
5 Didn't make the grade
6 Clear as a bell
7 Fateful day in March
8 Bird beak
9 Rocky spot
10 Send in different directions
11 God of discord and mischief
12 German automaker
13 Feeling one's oats
19 Dayspring direction
24 View from Marseille
25 Sends a letter
26 Maroon's locale, perhaps
27 Smallest possible

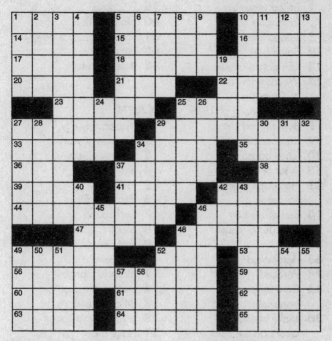

28 Church part
29 Fishy or fishing stories
30 Perennial herb or clergyman's headdress
31 Top bunk
32 Letter openers
34 Rutherford or Helen
37 Beatles album
40 Extensive properties
42 Make a choice
43 Promoters
45 Big book

46 Hook for cutting grass
48 Kind of energy
49 Up to the job
50 Float used to mark channels
51 Europe's highest volcano
52 Orange skin
54 Highlight for Sills
55 Smallest of the litter
57 Electronics brand
58 Fortify

LOOKIE, LOOKIE

ACROSS

1 Bread pieces, to fondue
5 Tempts fate
10 Small building
14 "En garde" weapon
15 Words with "care" or "mind"
16 Screen pooch of 1939
17 Built on request
19 Responsibility
20 Chewbacca
22 A lot of noise
23 Hogwarts postal carrier
24 Box office buy
28 Wander aimlessly
30 Poke
33 Actor Milo
34 Parched
35 Campaigner's barometer
36 Make mental errors on the field
39 Pigs' digs
40 Word with T or dry
41 Kent portrayer
42 Mach 1 breaker
43 Benches, not stenches
44 Animosity
45 Smile shape
46 AA applicant
47 Tenacious individual
55 Dancer at a disco
56 Luxurious situation
58 Check
59 ___ nous
60 Go ballistic
61 "So what ___ is new?"
62 Put away
63 It smells a lot

DOWN

1 Moderately dry
2 Orchestral work
3 Cutworm, e.g.
4 Stiff bristle
5 Idiot
6 Pitch producer
7 Surf sound
8 Means' justification
9 Fret about
10 Pub perch
11 Motorist's protest
12 Decorative case
13 Bit of reality?
18 Trying experience
21 Have bills
24 Trading card company
25 Elba and Aruba
26 "Dee-fense!," e.g.
27 Accordion parts
28 Virginia dances
29 Kind of surgery
30 It's often wild
31 Wanted poster word of old
32 Run in the wash
34 Present unfairly

35 Sonneteer
37 Freezer output
38 Figure of speech?
43 Person who plays for work
44 Walked (with "it")
45 Make reparation
46 Arena posting
47 Shrek, for one
48 Holiday song
49 Sponsorship
50 Actress Rowlands

51 Modern Sony offering
52 Alternative rock group
53 Golfer Aoki
54 Med. brain scans
57 "Told you so!"

PROBLEMS AHEAD

ACROSS

1 Cotton seed pod
5 Individual
10 Confession confessions
14 Vicinity
15 City on the Ruhr
16 Medicinal plant
17 Difficult spot
20 The first of September?
21 Cultivates, perhaps
22 Cliburn's instrument
23 Tailless feline
24 Not as spicy
26 Show up
29 Pirate treasure
30 "Cannery Row" character
31 Spiral-shelled gastropod
32 Dombey's partner
35 Bit of a brouhaha
39 Say "Cheese," maybe
40 Hack's passengers
41 Comes to the rescue
42 Worked diligently
43 Respectful gesture
45 Rabbit ears
48 Towel word
49 Inclination
50 Starship hit
51 Hardwood variety
54 Between a rock and a hard place
58 Piece of fencing?
59 Paycheck
60 It might wind up on a lake?
61 Geeky guy
62 Clear the board
63 Henry VIII's second wife

DOWN

1 Pedestal part
2 Scraps that Spot gets into
3 Souvenirs with scents
4 Lancelot du ___ (knight of the Round Table)
5 Over and above
6 English county on the Thames
7 Egyptian goddess
8 Shrimp snare
9 Large African antelope
10 Lustrous and smooth
11 Story of Achilles
12 Nary a soul
13 Tijuana title
18 Mongol chieftain
19 Unconcern
23 Malicious
24 Adherences
25 Out of one's mind
26 Rodin sculpture
27 Bean curd food
28 Math course, for short
29 Showed obsequiousness

31 Nuclear reactor parts
32 Word with monkey or birthday
33 Race track figures
34 Meddlesome
36 Some score notes
37 Flag Alex Rieger's vehicle
38 Galley gear
42 Held to the mat
43 Cherry red
44 Asian range

45 Drained of color
46 Split to unite
47 Not as well-done
48 Charon's underworld
50 The Forsytes had one
51 Sign for a seeress
52 Last word in Bibles
53 Leafy greens
55 IOU component
56 Kind of cry
57 Historic time

LOGICAL PICK

ACROSS

1 Causes of some spinning wheels
5 Tiny creature
10 "Hey, you!"
14 "___ go bragh"
15 Emitted coherent light
16 Words with "the minute" and "date"
17 Twin to Jacob
18 1969 Hitchcock film
19 Separate
20 PICK
23 Motor attachment?
24 Tell's home canton
25 Word with cut or bill
27 Big name in Top 40
29 Fleshy fruit
32 Doc bloc
33 Animal named for its coat color
36 Double curve
37 PICK
40 Girl of kiddie literature
41 Eminem, e.g.
42 Fingers
43 "For Once ___ Life"
44 Colorful parrot
48 Deadly
50 Quilting party
52 Attorneys' org.
53 PICK
58 Disorderly groups
59 Flat agreement
60 Carrier to Ben-Gurion
61 Occupy the throne
62 Frenzied
63 Twelve zeroes prefix
64 Leave be
65 Troutlike fish
66 Small whirlpool

DOWN

1 Shoe named for an antelope
2 Sea witch in "The Little Mermaid"
3 Bridal shop section
4 A bit tight
5 Hitching post?
6 New Zealand native
7 Catch sight of
8 Necklace unit
9 Wood trimmer
10 Class member
11 Like the Jetson's house
12 Party decoration
13 Preschooler
21 "Serpico" director Sidney
22 DVD player alternative
26 Dundee denial
28 Pennsylvania port
29 Full of energy
30 Slippery critters
31 In ___ (stuck)
34 "Phooey!"
35 1/8 fluid ounce

36 Gumbo pod
37 Social butterfly
38 Volatile
39 Caravan transport
40 Skippy rival
43 Type
45 Summoned
46 On the train
47 Ambush
49 Balance sheet plus
50 Pesto ingredient
51 Put in office

54 "Desire Under the ___"
55 Flyers, for one
56 Curse
57 Rose known as "Charlie Hustle"
58 "___ Doubtfire"

BELOW THE JOINT

ACROSS

1 "Do the ___"
5 Showy display
10 Answered a charge
14 A lot, for many?
15 Execution loop
16 Like a Monday crossword
17 Bad review
19 Get high
20 Part of WYSIWYG
21 Ron Howard's high school classmate Rene
22 Duck down
23 Word with east or date
24 Wood sorrels
26 Dali's country
29 Sign of agreement
34 Nervous thing in a room full of rocking chairs?
36 Actor elected president
37 Public panic
38 Fist fight
40 Simpson imp
41 Sound attachment
43 Less attractive
45 Hand-held device
47 Funny guy Bruce
48 Font selection
49 Seller's postings
50 Subject of Montezuma
53 Silk with a wavy pattern

56 Vent starter
59 In the area
60 Green olives, baby pickles, etc.
62 Lady of the knight?
63 Susan of "Baywatch"
64 Jamaican hybrid fruit
65 Husky load
66 Shopping hub of old Athens
67 Shed, as skin

DOWN

1 Bath and welcome
2 Lumbago, e.g.
3 Dead on target
4 It may be around a woman's knees
5 Follow an event
6 North Atlantic food fishes
7 Water closets in London
8 In a faint
9 Gymnast's reward
10 Some refrigerator contents
11 Word with off or into
12 "To be," to Brutus
13 Color changer
18 Main impact
22 Simplicity
23 Ill-humored
25 Type of drive
26 Leftover piece of iron
27 Monetary unit of India

28 Ring around
a lagoon
29 Move quickly
30 Even if, shortened
31 Once more
32 Singing Carpenter
33 Log line
35 Butcher's jelly
39 Two-year-old
42 "Roots," for one
44 Senior church official
46 Crippling

49 Sports building
50 Common conjunctions
51 Get-up-and-go
attribute
52 Broken to the saddle
54 "___ victory!"
55 Stravinsky or Sikorsky
56 Jumping stick
57 Throw the dice
58 Mince words?
60 Air-traffic agcy.
61 Fi fo follower

MAID SERVICE

ACROSS

1 Code crackers' comments
5 Cottonwood covering
9 Gunslinger's command
14 Phnom ___, Cambodia
15 Many a toy train track
16 Atlanta school
17 Prik king cuisine
18 Opera box
19 Equipped to eavesdrop
20 Man with lots of power
23 Century plant's rarity
25 Gymnast's reward
26 Toil and trouble
27 It has an area of about 69 sq. miles
32 Income sharer (Abbr.)
33 Relatively safe military position
34 Mast attachment
38 Café ___ (black coffee)
40 Tickle one's funny bone
43 Philosopher Descartes
44 Yogic position
46 1969 World Series champs
48 Bellum's opposite
49 Investment device
53 Big bird
56 Roman candle path
57 Sudden feelings
58 "Billy Bathgate" star
63 Eskimo word for "Eskimo"
64 Fairy-tale monster
65 Mane site
68 Word with horse or free
69 Enthusiastic vigor
70 Strain at a ___
71 Did some cobbling
72 Put on cloud nine
73 Sicilian spouter

DOWN

1 Well-chosen
2 "They'll never suspect me!"
3 Museum in 27-Across
4 Civil War battle
5 Weight-laden lasso
6 The Bard of ___
7 Pasta sauce brand
8 Compulsive shoplifter, slangily
9 Goes back to the start
10 Release, in a way
11 Angiogram image
12 Dogma
13 Kind of foil or power
21 Any son of Fatima
22 One with a nest egg
23 African title of respect
24 Nigeria's principal city
28 World's largest professional org.
29 Shapely limb, slangily

30 Outdo
31 EMT's treatment
35 Detestable
36 Vapid
37 Books
39 ER employees
41 It may swell or have swells
42 Odds and ends abbreviation
45 Expected
47 Pond refuse
50 East or West trailer

51 Resounds
52 Color on Ireland's flag
53 Tosses out a line?
54 Author Alice or H.H.
55 Type of suspects
59 Word with crimson or high
60 Leer lasciviously
61 Friend of Kukla
62 Stave (off)
66 Barrie boy
67 SFO stat

CAPITAL GUYS

ACROSS

1 Area of corporate investment, briefly
6 Blue flag, for one
10 Brown truck co.
13 "___ all ye faithful . . ."
14 Science fiction, say
16 It comes before view or text
17 Wrestling capital?
19 Garden implement
20 Helios, to the Romans
21 Aristotle's instructor
22 Assemblage
24 Return's home?
25 Velvet finish
26 Fleece
27 "Sesame Street" capital
32 Warn
35 Desire
36 Smallest prime number
37 Spy
38 Sworn body
40 Root veggie
41 Some cubes
42 Short personal histories
43 Supported
44 Hollywood capital?
48 Rara ___
49 Fond du ___
50 Bruce or Robert
53 Hammed it up
55 A Duke's cousin
57 Hockey legend
58 Miss Piggy's question
59 Country capital?
62 Groom's reply
63 Loma ___, Calif.
64 River Aire city
65 "Roseanne" character
66 A little salt
67 Heron

DOWN

1 Big name in vermouth
2 Boards treader
3 Yuletide strains
4 Org. with tags
5 Most inscrutable
6 Tropical lizard
7 Take a breather
8 Keen on
9 ___ Lanka
10 Give padding and cover?
11 Boat front
12 Rank
15 Cipher
18 "The Black Stallion" boy
23 French king
26 Remuneration
27 Mineral
28 Actress Rene

29 Married woman
30 Notable Meany
31 A, B, C or D
32 Middle Eastern prince
33 Sets of graph points
34 Mile, for Denver
38 Domino dots
39 ___-la-la
40 Fight with fists
42 Shower type
43 Kid's transport
45 Snake target

46 Hebrew prophet
47 Shuttle org.
50 Also-ran
51 Wear away
52 Dadaism co-founder
53 In the middle of
54 Musical conclusion
55 Funny Carvey
56 No ifs, ___ or
     buts . . .
60 Chapeau
61 Bash barrel

LESSON LEARNED

ACROSS

1 Small amphibians
5 S&L insurer
9 Window frame
13 Public upheaval
14 Orange exteriors
16 Entreaty
17 Word defined by 61-Across
19 Barley brews
20 Whale groups
21 Postal matter
23 "Dr. No" star Andress
26 Ivan the Terrible, for one
27 Lass
28 Start of the definition of 17-Across
31 Outback roamer
32 Grasp
33 Hit the slopes
34 Majestic
37 Packed away
39 Mischievous
43 Legendary flier
45 Stopover in la mer
47 Commotion
48 End of the definition
54 Camel hair coat
55 Kilmer subject
56 Cheap-looking
57 Rock singer Etheridge
59 Swine with tusks
60 Produced

61 Author of the definition
66 Watered down, so to speak
67 Awaken
68 House calls?
69 Mitigate
70 "The Untouchables" crimefighter Eliot
71 Telescope part

DOWN

1 Before, in rhyme
2 Quandary
3 Take this out for a spin
4 Accelerate
5 Vacation starters, often
6 Bites the dust
7 Wayfarer's shelter
8 Record holder's replacement?
9 Sail support
10 Charge
11 Vacillate
12 Imbroglio
15 Some chairs
18 Teacher's list
22 English explorer
23 Person on a terminal
24 Frost
25 Self-pleased
26 Frequent request
29 Colonists' castoff

30 Wire measure
35 "Where the Wild Things ___"
36 Plunders
38 Yalie
40 Charlatan
41 "Julius Caesar" date
42 Prying
44 Position locator
46 Goes along with
48 Risky move

49 Spain plus Portugal
50 Some hotel workers
51 Determining factor
52 Get friendlier
53 Rabbit ears
58 Paris notion
59 Paul Robeson, for one
62 Pool gear
63 Strong alkali
64 Lair
65 It's in front of the tee

PUZZLE WITHOUT A POINT

ACROSS

1 They're positioned in the church
5 Word with "top" (army bigwigs)
10 Word with top (jacket)
14 Type of surgeon
15 Word with top (first-rate)
16 Word with top (head covers)
17 Irish republic
18 Each
19 Bear in the sky
20 Is a Nosy Parker
22 Less encumbered
23 Red Sox legend Williams
24 Capitol and others
27 Old Testament book
30 Boca ___, Florida
31 Look here to see the world
32 Energy source
33 Day title word
37 Cap-a-pie
40 They get picked up at bars
41 Vitamin unit
42 "Rad!"
43 Zellweger of "Chicago"
44 Backs off (with "up")
45 It's a snap
49 Eggs partner
50 Calcutta coin
51 Plods (along)

55 Persia, since 1935
56 Wiser companion
59 Giants manager Felipe
60 Acquire, as through a trade
61 Bakery need
62 Word with share or bomb
63 "More," to Browning
64 They separate fair from foul
65 What mobsters pack

DOWN

1 Cummings attraction?
2 Where Perry prevailed
3 Beaver's father
4 Iditarod participants
5 Drain the brakes
6 Guns the engine
7 Hail, to Caesar
8 Sun. speech
9 Cunning
10 Make butter
11 Competed at Henley
12 Between ports
13 Peter and Paul
21 Last but not ___
22 Games companion
24 Deadly snake
25 Star of "The Ruling Class"
26 ___ of the Unknown Soldier
27 Bowie knife handle, e.g.
28 Other, to a Spaniard

29 Oscar Madison, for one
30 Pillage and plunder
33 Sauna alternative
34 JFK postings
35 By ___ (from memory)
36 Andy's partner
38 Unoccupied, as country
39 Early hour
43 "Riddle-me-___" ("Guess!")
45 Lace ruffle

46 Distinctive qualities
47 Reaches across
48 Works the garden
49 Inflics pain
51 ___ majesty
52 Romanian-born novelist Wiesel
53 Capital of Italia
54 Tallow source
56 Popeye's Olive ___
57 Maui necklace
58 Rock's Steely ___

DON'T GET PUSHY

ACROSS

1 How to say "hurry up" in a hurry
5 Shell out
10 "The ___ of Katie Elder"
14 "Bobby" co-star Moore
15 Nobelist of 1903
16 Come together
17 Butler's last word?
18 City on the Mohawk
19 Italian volcano
20 Auto shop worker
23 Heavenly instrument
24 Disallow
25 To wit
28 "I ___ to recall . . ."
30 Links number
33 Farewell abroad
34 Contemporary of Louis and Duke
35 Melchior et al.
36 Exert one's influence
39 Wapitis
40 Bona ___
41 Destroy a bow
42 Shoat's home
43 Red ___ (newts)
44 Gets a smile out of
45 Sure-footed domesticated mammal
46 Spheres
47 Some competitions
54 Carry on
55 Blood line
56 Passe preposition
58 Party to
59 Street urchin
60 Ananias, for one
61 Ice cream purchase
62 Ordain
63 Upper hand

DOWN

1 Append
2 It's sought after in Washington
3 Chamber stock
4 Windblown toys
5 Rush
6 Provide with lodgings
7 Famous redhead
8 Christmas saint
9 Human sponge
10 Unit of wound thread
11 Airing
12 Muse count
13 Hollywood Walk of Fame figure
21 Anklebone
22 Saint rival
25 Scruffs
26 Stage of growth
27 Cloudy
28 Inuit transports
29 "What ___ can I say?"
30 They have seats
31 College Station athlete

32 Attains status
34 Discharge
35 Tiny
37 Behind the scenes
38 Cuban dance
43 Serpentine curve
44 Downright
45 Deputy
46 Sight-related
47 Tiresome one
48 Asian royal
49 Bath's river

50 Reddish horse
51 Cookery's Rombauer
52 "National Velvet" author Bagnold
53 Alone at the prom
57 Fraction of a krone

BODY BAG

ACROSS

1 Like some lettuce
5 Went downhill, in a way
10 Alley targets
14 Enjoying the QEII
15 Man on a mission
16 Stir turbulently
17 Wine press residue
18 Had a home-cooked meal
19 Nothing but
20 Onerous
23 German is taught here
24 It should be raised in the office
28 Brazil-Paraguay border river
29 Former kiwi kin
32 Overhauled
33 Swing and miss three times
35 Scary
38 "Shall we?"
40 Sinuous
41 Cornell's ___ Hall
42 Political pressure
45 H.S.T. running mate
46 It's fit for a queen
47 Boy toy
48 Dubya classmate
50 Potent bridge pair
52 Mental cases
55 Rhythmically lively
59 Star warrior
62 Coasts on thermals
63 Thames town
64 Last word of the Bible
65 Gold unit
66 Debussy's "Clair de ___"
67 Step up
68 Hasn't, but should have
69 Diving bird

DOWN

1 Sacrificial offerings
2 Mathematician Newton
3 Trading vessel
4 Prepare to leave, in a way
5 It's picked up in the alley
6 Shakespeare's shrew
7 It's a thought
8 The phantom of the opera
9 Strauss material
10 Get somewhere
11 It's attractive and has a charge
12 It's nothing
13 Weaselly
21 Ho-hum
22 Me neither
25 Without limit
26 Like a musical staff
27 Tool put away for the winter

29 Capital of Belarus
30 Wax eloquent
31 Actor Alan or Adam
33 Scruggs' partner
34 Cliff dwelling
36 "___ was going to St. Ives . . ."
37 Writer Rand
39 Raking with gunfire
43 Chisholm Trail town
44 Microbe
49 Fashionable flaps

51 Rose red dye
52 Goes for
53 Words with two or hole
54 Ford predecessor
56 Manner of speaking
57 Wise guy
58 Took a hike
59 Deliver a hard hit to
60 It'll never get off the ground
61 Domestic retreat

BRUSH UP

ACROSS

1 Church fixture
6 Chianti, e.g.
10 Asst., for one
14 Lead-and-tin alloy
15 Tied
16 Place for a honey bunch?
17 Environmentalist's concern
19 Pulitzer winner of 1958
20 Debaters, essentially
21 Tries to bribe a jury, perhaps
23 Regions
25 Penitent one
26 Strolls leisurely
29 Set of clothes
31 Misfortune
34 Modern Greece's legislative assembly
35 "Someone ___ Dream" (Faith Hill)
36 Suffix with rigor
37 Word with cheeks or outlook
38 Culpability
39 Pipkins
40 Kind of can
41 "Saturday Night Fever" milieu
42 Podge attachment
43 Funnyman Brooks
44 "Dedicated to the ___ Love"
45 School assignment
46 Israeli leader Barak
48 Ages and ages
50 Ensnared
53 OK, informally
57 Louie De Palma's office setting
58 1942 Sabu flick
60 Air conditioner units
61 Viva voce
62 "When ___ You" (Irving Berlin)
63 Have a session
64 Stage star Neuwirth
65 100,000 in a newton

DOWN

1 Big name in razors
2 "Maude" producer Norman
3 Advanced math
4 Once a year
5 Ring authority
6 Vice ___
7 "___ Got You Under My Skin"
8 Bird's-___ soup
9 Precise
10 Mold
11 He's responsible for long drives
12 State
13 Eighteen on a course
18 Taconite and tinstone
22 State of confusion or disorder
24 Pt. of the British West Indies

26 Sarai's mate
27 Large ruminant
28 Second-rate
30 Christiania, today
32 Income's antithesis
33 Ruhr industrial center
35 The life of Riley
38 College graduate's goal, perhaps
39 Perhaps
41 Ill-humored

42 Actor Paul of "Casablanca"
45 Recline
47 1952 Eniwetok event
49 American symbol
50 Subject of SALT
51 Hoopster Archibald
52 Simple partner?
54 Hired thug
55 Running attire?
56 Some adv. purchases
59 Capture, as a fugitive

SAUCED

ACROSS

1 Alternative to raspberries
5 Gladiator's protection
11 Deli favorite
14 Come up against
15 Genghis Khan follower
16 Zsa Zsa's sister
17 In a passionate manner
19 "Wolfman" portrayer Chaney Jr.
20 Outer layer of seeds
21 Piedmont wine center
22 Disown
23 John Dos Passos trilogy
25 Jazz saxophonist Getz
27 Best
34 El Dorado's treasure
35 Unadulterated
36 Henley boat
37 Lively dance
40 Busy person's alleged work load
41 ___ Hawkins
42 Type of political campaign
43 Gardenia or lilac
45 Movie format
46 New baby, often
50 Shakespeare's King
51 ___ Na Na
52 "Woe is me!"
54 Dusseldorf denial
58 Bandleader Shaw
62 86,400 seconds
63 Binding, as a contract
65 Hwy. crosser
66 No more than
67 Humerus connector
68 Damage
69 Measure of success, for some
70 Response to "Shall we?"

DOWN

1 Bangkok coin
2 Wind with a wide range
3 Pop-ups, usually
4 Jean Antoine Houdon creation
5 Avg.
6 Laugh track refrain
7 Furies
8 Coup d'___
9 Luxuriant
10 Kind of cell or wall
11 "I Am Woman" woman
12 Stratford-on-___
13 Lots and lots
18 LEM agency
22 Russian villa
24 Hi-fi component
26 Hardy heroine
27 Charley horse
28 Psychotherapy patient, at times

Puzzle 57

29 "___ Africa"
30 Tolkien character
31 Mortise insertion
32 Martini garnish
33 Addressed the court
34 Greek peak
38 Macy's specials
39 Kind of code
44 ___ judicata (decided case)
47 Elaborately adorned
48 Herring

49 Sharp rebuke
52 First of all?
53 Etna output
55 Humorist Bombeck
56 It may be false
57 Political cartoonist Thomas
59 Story by Chaucer
60 "___ that special?"
61 JFK postings
63 "Hee ___"
64 Last in a series

IT BELONGS TO HER

ACROSS

1 Up-tempo jazz style
6 Up and about
11 II
14 Shelley's "Popeye" role
15 Knightly
17 Blame for a woman?
19 "Howards ___," Forster novel
20 Literary composition
21 Mark for omission
22 Scottish caps
23 English general
26 Figure of speech
29 Jumping frog creator
30 Eastern mountain range
31 Field partner
32 Wrath
35 Woman's arcanum?
39 Orlando-to-Miami dir.
40 Abandon
41 Allow to borrow
42 Full of meaning
43 Docket
45 Theatrical performance
48 He works for the lord
49 Rising locale?
50 Burn soother
51 Signal of a sort
54 Woman's resort?

59 In bridge, diamonds or clubs
60 From Scandinavia
61 Yankovic and Roker
62 Molts
63 African country

DOWN

1 Table wine
2 Spiritedness
3 Tough situation
4 Reproductive cells
5 Snail mail buddy
6 Field measures
7 Noah's oldest
8 ___ Maria (coffee liqueur)
9 Hospital administrators? (Abbr.)
10 HRM's fliers
11 More genuine
12 Estate papers
13 Eight performers
16 Burdened
18 Capitol topper
22 Pinball mishap
23 Inundated
24 PC counterparts
25 Cost increase
26 Rodeos and Pathfinders
27 Eye part
28 Liquid defense
29 Singer-songwriter Chapman

Puzzle 58

31 Ten percent offering
32 Atomic number 26
33 Interpret
34 Sicilian volcano
36 Norse deity
37 Religious ceremony
38 Musical notation
42 Bean type
43 Long time
44 Golf destinations?
45 Mell Lazarus strip
46 Service

47 Sea swallows
48 Narrow incisions
50 Eager
51 Check someone's ID
52 ___ Major
   (Great Bear)
53 Paradise
55 "48 ___" (1982)
56 Wednesday preceder
   once a year
57 Litigate
58 Current solver

OFF TO THE RACES

ACROSS

1 Dangerous reptile
4 Mail org.
8 Acknowledges
   with one's fedora
13 "___ desperandum"
   (Horace)
14 Bowler's 7-10, e.g.
15 Florida citrus center
16 Barely achieve
   (with "out")
17 George's brother
19 Bric-a-brac stand
21 Takes umbrage
22 Formerly
23 Radio station sign
24 Place to haggle
28 Important time,
   history-wise
31 Off-Broadway
   theater award
32 Instant greenery
33 Missing-person locator
35 Fatty compound
37 Highly reliable evidence
39 Range
40 Handsome young man
42 Stowe's little heroine
44 Zeno's birthplace
45 Stimpy's cartoon buddy
46 Classroom diversion
49 They may be
   locked or blown
50 Brewed drink
51 Attire
54 Not deep at all

58 Certain researcher
60 Pub potion
61 "The Canterbury
   Tales" pilgrim
62 Second or sixth president
63 One getting the
   red carpet treatment
64 Canadian physician
   Sir William
65 Turner and Cole
66 Picnic problem

DOWN

1 "There's ___ day
   dawning . . ."
2 Punjabi believer
3 "Guilty," e.g.
4 Displaces
5 Blinds crosspiece
6 Snowball in
   "Animal Farm"
7 Breastbones
8 Some FBI files
9 Fall color
10 Kowtow
11 Dart
12 Without
14 Scorch
18 Do a double-take, e.g.
20 Absorb
23 Been there, done that
24 Grinding tooth
25 Tolerate
26 Wisconsin college
   town and college

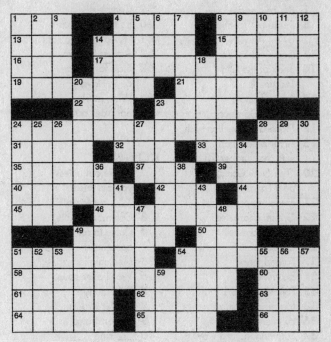

27 Peas' place
28 Eleve's place
29 Drive back
30 "He's ___ nowhere man" (Beatles)
34 Perfume ingredient
36 Chaos
38 Clark's "Mogambo" co-star
41 Hag
43 National songs

47 Temporarily at the museum
48 Hons
49 Split
51 Dr. J wore one
52 Slapstick-movie missiles
53 Rind
54 Game with 32 cards
55 Magma exposed
56 Actress Lena
57 Turned on the waterworks
59 Nutritional advisory, abbr.

THE JAYCEES CLUB

ACROSS

1 8th of a series
6 Reese of "Touched by an Angel"
11 Comment by Scrooge
14 Book of the Old Testament
15 An archangel
16 Actress Gardner
17 Make a connection with
18 Actor associated with the number 23
20 "The New Colossus" poet Lazarus
21 French impressionist
22 Grimm character
23 French farewell
25 Capsizes
27 Famed tenor
31 Examine
32 Folk singer Burl
33 Morning moisture
36 Highlander
37 Summoned, in a way
39 Golfer's target
40 Part of CBS (Abbr.)
41 Star of "Elephant Boy"
42 Hangman's knot
43 Author of "Lord Jim"
46 Learned scholar
49 Extra charge
50 Former Federal Reserve chief Greenspan
51 Infuse
54 Blow from a cat-o'-nine-tails
57 He played a Corleone
59 Completely
60 It's for the Byrds
61 "Keep your ___ on!"
62 Actress Burstyn
63 Stats for Oscar de la Hoya
64 Whip marks
65 Sprinkles powder

DOWN

1 You're out unless you put this in
2 "___ to please!"
3 Common people
4 Come to an agreement
5 Medical plan gp.
6 Word after soup.
7 Emerald Isle
8 Gimlet sweetener
9 Remonstrated
10 ___ king
11 Flat-bottomed vessel
12 Prevent
13 19th U.S. president
19 "Friends" character
21 ___ culpa
24 Glacial
26 Faux ___
27 Sharp projections
28 "___ can you see . . ."
29 Construct haphazardly
30 Second of all?

Puzzle 60

33 Entranceway fasteners
34 Lanchester of "The Bride of Frankenstein"
35 Garden intruder
37 Incongruous composition
38 Lincolnesque nickname
39 Aloha State capital
41 Cain was the first
42 Sign of approval
43 Tarzan's mate
44 Former hangouts

45 Alphabet trio
46 Host of "Wheel of Fortune"
47 It fell in 1836
48 Improvised musical accompaniments
52 Camelot coat
53 Simpson lad
55 Editor's notation
56 Old biddies
58 Wind dir.
59 Proof-ending abbr.

NUMBERING SYSTEM

ACROSS

1 Well-publicized shindig
5 Voting-machine lists
11 R.M.N.'s predecessor
14 "Me too" response
15 March event
16 Choler
17 Odd couple, or dead ends?
18 Military band?
19 "Out!" from an Okie
20 Portable shade?
23 Patronized, as a diner
26 School address abbr.
27 Extreme prefix
28 Loud welcome?
31 Beach brief
32 ___ Luis Obispo
33 It has shoulders but no head
37 PC key
38 Second of all?
40 Part of a matching set, sometimes
42 Song syllable
43 Part of CBS or DOS
45 Bank alternative, briefly
47 Scented sample
49 Podunk, proverbially?
52 Battle of 1836
55 Compass dir.
56 "Oui" and "si"
57 Gambler's choice

60 Electronics brand
61 Military command
62 Worshipper's locale, sometimes
66 Pained reactions
67 Make hermetic
68 Thespian's gig
69 Command to Benji
70 Hunt and Hayes
71 Barbershop job

DOWN

1 Convertible, after conversion
2 Serve brilliantly
3 Ursula Andress film
4 SWAT team rescuee
5 Bridge
6 Big T-shirts
7 Battle groups
8 Actress Bankhead
9 Pulitzer-winning biographer Leon
10 Embark, as on a journey
11 Feathery
12 Prickly plant
13 Beetle alternative
21 Chopin piece
22 NY Met, for example
23 Beasts of burden
24 Intoxicated
25 Boardroom VIPs
29 Stars that brighten then fade

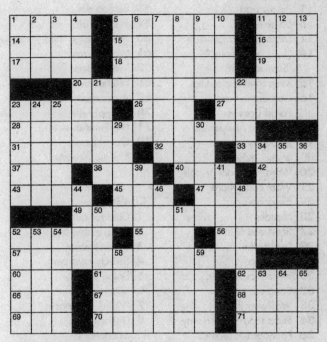

30 College class hours
34 Preminger and Klemperer
35 "___ there yet?"
36 Mends
39 Heavenly
41 "Later"
44 Big volume
46 Carter's running mate
48 "Maggie May" singer Rod
50 What the driver carries?

51 What the planet Krypton orbited
52 Spherical hairdos
53 Chinese fruit
54 Nautical "Halt!"
58 Suits to ___
59 Agts.
63 The "F" in FYI
64 Boxing winner in Zaire, 1974
65 "The One I Love" group

IN SEASON

ACROSS

1 Arrow part
6 Some files
11 Did not stand for it?
14 "I ___ Symphony," (Supremes hit)
15 Keep from happening
16 One of the Four Forest Cantons
17 Post-thaw restlessness
19 Election-year ammo, maybe
20 Word with boot or pole
21 Wool coat wearer
22 Executive's deg.
23 Maudlin
27 Short end of the stick
29 Lord of the ring, once
30 Twice-monthly tide
32 Bring up, as kids
33 Way over there
34 Sticks together, in a way
36 Phonograph records
39 Aware of
41 Maze word
43 Red's meaning, at times
44 Holders of many frames
46 Spud
48 Lord's Prayer opener
49 Descartes the mathematician
51 Founder of Time and Life
52 Bean counter, for short
53 Apt to break

56 Janitor's aid
58 Surfing site
59 Part of TGIF
60 Hawaiian garland
61 Wall St. deal
62 World Series
68 Feather mate
69 Arctic shelter
70 Dubya's wife
71 Nightmarish street
72 Out of humor
73 Chilling forecast

DOWN

1 Calls for quiet
2 Cool, in the '50s
3 Bernese flower
4 Search, as a perp
5 Doing horribly
6 Spitfire org.
7 "Hail!" to Horace
8 Discontinue, as relations
9 Period prior to 1941, in the U.S.
10 Scattered about
11 Certain theater productions
12 Caribbean paradise
13 Pertaining to neap and ebb
18 MacKenzie of "Your Hit Parade"
23 "Key to the City" presenter

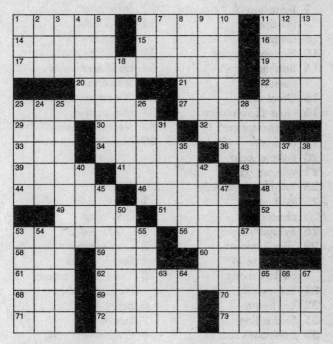

24 Having no company
25 Something school kids hope for in December?
26 Stamping ground
28 Place for roasting
31 "He loves me" piece
35 Deceptive scheme
37 Two-door vehicle
38 Fine drops of water
40 Table tub
42 Carmaker's woe
45 Kick the bucket

47 Closes again, as an envelope
50 Infuriate
53 Come together
54 Sherpa's home
55 Some pickles, familiarly
57 Hemp fiber
63 Studio site
64 Affectedly modest
65 Seek redress
66 It makes one hot
67 One familiar with litter

ENTERTAINING CENTER

ACROSS

1 Kurosawa of the cinema
6 Carpet type
10 Norwegian saint
14 Brits' floor coverings
15 Grant name
16 Naldi of silent films
17 Carburetor part
19 Mild oath
20 Actress Locke
21 48-card game
23 Talk about endlessly
25 Was worthy of notice
26 Syllogist's word
29 Thee, updated
30 First name in old talk shows
31 Eat greedily
33 Bar fixture
35 Stud setting
38 Loses one's cool
40 Get popular all over
42 Jamaican music
43 Fountain selections
45 Follow
46 Fearsome creature of old, briefly
48 Word with down, key or blow
50 Notary's tool
51 Hammer on a bench
53 Hat made from jipijapa
55 Social bias
57 Takes after
61 1953 Leslie Caron film
62 Apple has one
64 Old French coins
65 Take on cargo
66 "Goodnight ___"
67 Mile portions
68 Meadow moms
69 Church council

DOWN

1 Landon and a TV alien
2 1,000 to start?
3 ___ the ground floor
4 Selfish drivers
5 "Ad ___ per aspera" (Kansas motto)
6 Sauna site
7 Lend a hand
8 Chipmunk of song
9 Narrow valley
10 Kind of garage
11 Limerick, e.g.
12 "___ of Two Cities"
13 Less colorful
18 Diversify
22 Threat ending
24 Sat for a portrait
26 Spawn
27 Corner piece
28 A steal
30 A Howard

32 Canvas supports
34 Welles of film
36 Rio contents
37 Line holder
39 Curse
41 Distasteful
44 Pie choice
47 Fend off
49 Float on the breeze
51 Staff leader?
52 One of the Kramdens
53 "I don't believe that!"

54 Song thrush
56 Minute land mass
58 "The Virginian"
author Wister
59 Clinton cabinet
member
60 Downhill conveyance
63 Legal thing

TABLE SETTING

ACROSS

1 Word in Einstein's equation
5 Ye ___ shoppe
9 Screenwriter Chayefsky
14 "Gymnopédies" composer Satie
15 Lowing places
16 Leave out
17 "Let Us Now Praise Famous Men" author James
18 Crazed
19 Eskimos' kissers?
20 "Do You Believe in Magic" band
23 Gregg specialist, for short
24 Blunt sword
25 Be decisive
28 Bowery bums
31 Draws out
33 Campgrounds residue
36 Jude or James
39 Ms. Teasdale
40 1962 Polanski film
44 Reckless
45 Land and sea meeting place
46 Curvy letter
47 Skater Baiul
50 Program command
52 Marshal of Waterloo
53 There are 54 in a game, usually
56 Okra soup

60 Decision spot
64 Gambler's loss, figuratively
66 Spaghetti sauce brand
67 Kind of van or bus
68 Cockney's challenge
69 Emerald Isle
70 Commodious crafts
71 Steep-walled land formations
72 Adept
73 Hatchling's home

DOWN

1 Square trio
2 In-group lingo
3 Colander kin
4 Coils of yarn
5 Automotive pioneer
6 Spring
7 Actor Willem
8 Prohibit legally
9 Like some fattened livestock
10 Baseball's Moises
11 Disjoint
12 H.S.T. successor
13 Conciliatory response
21 Lariat's end
22 Born
26 Shimon of Israel
27 Pre-Revolution leaders
29 Mai ___
30 Confessor's revelations
32 Superpower's letters

33 Ohio city
34 Grass inhabitant?
35 Whiny temper tantrums
37 Highest degree
38 Archaic pronoun
41 Agcy. for homeowners
42 East or West ending
43 Golf club
48 Some bridge positions
49 Shore bird
51 Words in a James
Coburn film title

54 Out of gas
55 Drum type
57 Watery-patterned
cloth
58 Safe places?
59 Keats or Milton, notably
61 Killer whale
62 End of the
work week letters
63 Peck partner
64 Uncle of 32-Down
65 Hurry

FAMOUS QUESTIONS

ACROSS
1 A way to consider
5 Pursue wild geese?
10 Slimy sci-fi menace
14 Sea lettuce
15 Titan, formerly
16 Cream-of-the-crop
17 ___ Cove, L.I.
18 Like some nail polish
19 "Follow me!"
20 Classic comedy
23 Pendulum's path
24 Much-used pencil
25 "Spring forward" letters
28 Spilled the beans
31 Footless
35 At the summit
37 Start of a Thomas Wolfe title
39 Singer Abdul
40 Good place for a green thumb
43 Cockamamie
44 French town of WWII fame
45 Where to find two black suits
46 Medicating
48 Reach across
50 Word with high or light
51 Pop singer Amos
53 Poet's pasture
55 Bank transaction for a geologist?

62 First place?
63 Mover's challenge
64 Osmatic stimulant
66 College book
67 Continental currency
68 When hands are at their highest point
69 Studio structures
70 Refine ore
71 Big game?

DOWN
1 Excavated (with "out")
2 Raines of old films
3 "Getting ___ With Dad" (Danson film)
4 Suffix with Wrestle
5 Classic product
6 Fanny or Benny
7 One of the acting Baldwins
8 Blackens
9 Novel flubs
10 Rim holder
11 Capital of Togo
12 ___ about (circa)
13 Cartwright and Franklin
21 "Rocky III" foe
22 Tea serving, in Britain
25 King of psalmists
26 Dictation taker

27 Roman wraps
29 Sampras shots
30 Not exactly Einsteins
32 Ranch hands
33 Smart guy
34 Gangling
36 Atoners
38 Edible seaweed
41 Highest natural adult male voice
42 Crossbar holder
47 Early wine?

49 New beginning
52 Latin name for Troy
54 In harmony
55 Subway Series team
56 ___ fixe (obsession)
57 On deck
58 Truth alternative
59 Chemical compound
60 Object of devotion
61 Commandeered
65 They may administer IVs

MY MOTTO IS . . .

ACROSS

1 Dershowitz of the bar
5 Gulf of California peninsula
9 Merit award
14 Edible Pacific tuber
15 Spanish pot
16 Goodbye in Gascony
17 New York state motto ("ever upward")
19 Plexus starter
20 "Hercules" spin-off
21 Calm
22 Dark brown
25 "From ___ shining . . ."
28 Shatner's war
29 High pt. in Sicily
31 The King's real first name
32 Hindu sacred text
33 Expos' ending
34 Wide-screen movie process
37 U.S. motto
41 Flowed copiously
42 "Blame it on ___" (Caine film)
44 Board game implement?
47 Whole shebang
48 High-class
50 "Now ___ seen everything!"
51 Window alternative
53 First name in photography
54 Legendary French knight
56 Try to tan
58 Topper
59 Montana motto ("gold and silver")
64 "Beau ___"
65 First-rate
66 Company VIP
67 Which cheek to turn?
68 Custodian's need
69 Editor's material

DOWN

1 Packed it away
2 Loose with the rules
3 Balfe's "Joan of ___"
4 Play by Jean-Paul Sartre
5 Cap'n's mate
6 False ID
7 Celeb in the news
8 Bern's river
9 Ezio Pinza, for one
10 Big commotions
11 Thin
12 Ready (with "up")
13 California motto ("I have found it!")
18 Request to a butcher
21 Some library tomes
22 School of Mustangs
23 Raison d'___
24 Use a chink
26 Size up

27 Gold, chemically
speaking
30 Reason to take shelter
32 Rental unit
35 First name in physics
36 Stinging nest builder
38 WWII landing craft
39 Sizable servers
40 Nichols or Wallace
43 Olive family name
44 Maine motto ("I direct")
45 Long-legged shore bird

46 Frank topping
49 Leg ornament
51 Ruffle one's feathers
52 Wood from Sri Lanka
55 Fixed bet
57 Verbal salutes
59 Bookshelf wood,
perhaps
60 Expensive eggs?
61 Log splitter
62 Cowhand's nickname
63 Don't hesitate

DRESS FOR SUCCESS

ACROSS

1 African capital
6 Epps, the actor
10 Sgt. Preston's grp.
14 Wood nymph
15 It's about 4,150 miles long
16 Author Wiesel
17 Book protection
19 Parent's warning
20 "Consummatum ___"
21 Peter Fonda role of '97
22 Debate subjects
24 Building on the beach
26 Put to the test
27 Be in control
32 Church part
35 ___ avis
36 Fury
37 Parts of mins.
38 Some are blind
40 "There's ___ day dawning . . ."
41 Debate side
42 Rash reaction?
43 Famed fed
44 Pompous person
49 Stadium levels
50 Deceived
54 Secret information
56 Dark, poetically
58 Bullring "bravo!"
59 Printer's blue-green
60 Metier
63 Cleopatra's love Antony
64 Beanery offering
65 Become allied
66 In ___ (existing)
67 Metal-stamping tools
68 Conundrum

DOWN

1 Common viper
2 Container for liquids
3 Liquid filled sacs
4 Hamelin evictee
5 Command earnestly
6 "For ___ in My Life" (Stevie Wonder)
7 Nichols or Wallace
8 Pub staple
9 Go on a pension
10 View from Jidda
11 Seventh heaven
12 Selfish one's exclamation
13 They may be collared
18 They have crosses to bear
23 Take tea
25 Hasn't ponied up
26 Island roof material
28 Fast waters
29 Harness races
30 Spanish crowd?
31 Keeps folks in stitches

32 Egyptian cobras
33 Feeling one's oats
34 Army reconnaissance transports
39 Israel's Peres
40 Garden soldiers
45 Ring bearer?
46 Swampland
47 Videotaped over
48 Register a sale?
51 Heavyweight champ from 1937–49

52 Ins
53 A way to discourage
54 Vertex
55 Certain thick-piled rugs
56 Noted Harper's Bazaar illustrator
57 Nickname for Springsteen
61 Mai ___ cocktail
62 ___-cone (summer treat)

UP HIGH

ACROSS

1 Haywire
5 Diner
10 Room in cyberspace
14 Brickmaker's furnace
15 Mosey
16 "Egad!" or "Drat!"
17 In search of whales
18 Rips off
19 Stead
20 CIA data, perhaps
23 July 1944 battle site
24 Ball chaser?
25 Coniferous trees
28 Teri of "Young Frankenstein"
30 Cat's dog?
33 Priestly vestment
34 Diamond corner
35 Laundry
36 Athlete's goal
39 Sea eagles
40 Put in a snit
41 Zeal
42 Sandwich choice
43 End of a saying from 43-Down
44 Compound of element number 5
45 Cray or pay ending
46 Juno, to the Greeks
47 Get-togethers for leaders
54 Lily family shrub
55 Words of honor?
56 Yellowfin, for one
58 Turf claimers
59 Calf catcher
60 Colonizer of Greenland
61 "Lonely Boy" singer
62 Oft-pressed key
63 Play for a fool

DOWN

1 Sobriquet preceder
2 Rainbow producer
3 Dairy case spread
4 Hikers' burdens
5 Supporters in the arts
6 It merged with BP in 1998
7 Aid for skiers
8 Sommer of films
9 An antique dealer, sometimes
10 Actor Firth
11 Damaging precipitation
12 To ___ (exactly)
13 Accordingly
21 Tonsillitis cousin
22 Advocating
25 Escapade
26 Nail smoother
27 Ladd of "28 Days"
28 Faux pas
29 Beginning on

Puzzle 68

30 Rare "bear"
31 Knotted neckwear
32 One of the five w's
34 Cheese with a rind
35 Justified
37 Prepare to fight
38 "Whale Rider" extra
43 Speaker of 43-Across
44 Croupier's customer
45 Last of a series
46 "Siddhartha" author

47 Lengthy tale
48 ___ Bator
49 Shalhoub series
50 Mournful cry
51 Bridge seat
52 Ashram figure
53 Scissors sound
57 Top pitcher

AMERICAN IDOL

ACROSS

1 Arm thugs, e.g.
5 Nuisance
9 Fundamentals
13 Multigenerational tale
14 Up-front amount
15 Memorable dieter
16 What fans called Frazier
18 Limber
19 Provide financial grants
20 Associate
21 Distress signal
24 Dennis or Doris
25 Gloved one
26 Rebounding sound waves
28 Vouchsafe
29 Alpine river
30 French cheese
31 Put-on
34 Avarice
35 Ship's record
36 Manner
38 Something to sniggle for
39 Elementary particle
40 Acadian Louisiana native
41 Veneration
44 British noblemen
45 Attacks verbally
47 Selvage
48 Squeeze (out)
49 Conned
50 Lots and lots
52 Pear variety

53 What fans called DiMaggio
57 Exclusive
58 Competent
59 Horse chow
60 No longer secret
61 Day's crest
62 "Who's Who" entries, briefly

DOWN

1 Hinny's relative
2 Emeril's "kick it up" shout
3 "I" affliction
4 Make off with
5 Asian bearlike mammals
6 Delight in
7 Pack
8 Strange prop?
9 Moon program
10 What fans called Namath
11 Hindu class
12 Guide
15 Icy precipitation
17 Most assuredly
20 Ascend
21 Maestro Koussevitzky
22 Yellow pigment
23 What fans called Jackson
25 Pretend
27 A number divided by itself is this

28 Witch transport
30 Type of music
32 Dull sound
33 Uptight
36 Large shrimp sauteed in oil
37 It's applied before feathers
39 Pinochle term
42 Western hangout
43 Traffic snarl
44 Defeated

45 Stockpile
46 From then till now
47 What Satchmo said to Dolly
50 Vagabond
51 Popinjay
53 LPGA member Stephenson
54 ___ Alai
55 Member of the Siouan people
56 Serpentine curve

REQUESTS

ACROSS

1 Call off, at Cape Canaveral
6 Coffee has a great one
11 Koppel of "Nightline"
14 Widow's interest in an estate
15 Italian-born French poet Christine de ___
16 Actress Merkel
17 Orleans request
19 Start of a dog star's name
20 WWII torpedo vessel
21 James' "Gunsmoke" co-star
23 Fifth Greek letter
26 Dangerous bacteria
27 Used a Gillette Mach 3
28 "The Shadow"
31 "Clan of the ___ Bear"
32 "Animal ___"
33 One of a pack?
34 ___-friendly
35 Complains peevishly
36 Recital numbers
37 Mich. city
38 ___ ease (uneasy)
39 Cruise and Selleck
40 Daytime Emmy-winning talk show host
42 Stops
44 Super stars?
45 Earthly
46 Like Bread's "Man"
48 Taxpayer's dread
49 Fraction of a joule
50 Elvis request
55 "___ Wednesday" (1973 film)
56 Jazz pianist Blake
57 Prudential rival
58 "King ___"
59 Sports data
60 Shooting sport

DOWN

1 Augment
2 Dressy wrap
3 Rent alternative
4 Randy Moss, for one
5 Tweeter output
6 Pertaining to bees
7 "Norma Rae" director
8 ___ Kosh B'Gosh (kids' clothing line)
9 One of the "Monday, Monday" singers
10 Relative of a buttercup
11 The Judds request
12 "National Velvet" author Bagnold
13 Comedian Carvey
18 "Ed ___" (Depp film)
22 Pacino and Capp
23 Portuguese coin
24 Discontinued, with "out"
25 Eagle-Eye Cherry request
26 Blow one's top

28 "King of the ___
    Sea" (1956)
29 Ewing and Getty, e.g.
30 Oder-___ Line
32 Actress/model Berry
35 Leave a place quickly
36 Roddenberry's show
38 Enters like an enemy
41 "Wayne's World"
    catchword
42 Sign away
43 Jong and Kane

45 "She's a Beauty"
    group (with "The")
46 Word with landing
    or second
47 "Superman II" villainess
48 "Look ___ this way, . . ."
51 Magic org.
52 Salt Lake team player
53 Hollywood-to-Death
    Valley dir.
54 Back muscle,
    to Billy Blanks

STARRING . . .

ACROSS

1 Falafel bread
5 Backbreaker, in a proverb
10 Wilbur Post's pet
14 Press agent?
15 Paper you can break
16 Top drawer
17 It may be due
18 Georgia of "The Mary Tyler Moore Show"
19 Start of an explanation
20 Unyielding
22 Laugh like the Wicked Witch
24 Wizards' foes
25 Dixieland jazz feature
26 Pungent root
29 "The Santa Clause" star
33 Hodgepodge or mishmash
34 Like some bloomers
35 Aldon of "The Barefoot Contessa"
36 Distinctive clothing
37 Patron saint of the lame
38 "No time to wallow in the ___" (Jim Morrison)
39 Blues legend James
40 Disagreeable responsibility
41 "Peter Pan" beast
42 Carrie Fisher's mom
44 Highest member of the violin family
46 Baby's favorite art movement?
47 Symbol of virtue
48 Surpassingly good
51 Palindromes may be read this way
55 Warsaw Pact country
56 Mary's "Little House" sister
58 New York canal opened in 1825
59 Painted Desert feature
60 Asked, and then some
61 Represent by drawing
62 Food, for Fido
63 Billiards stroke
64 Adjective for Jelly's Jam

DOWN

1 Berth place
2 "Dies ___" (Latin hymn)
3 Eighty-six
4 A Zorro
5 Magnifying glass carrier, stereotypically
6 Where some pitchers sleep
7 Over-the-top anger
8 Peer Gynt's mother
9 Invites in enthusiastically
10 "My Life So Far" star
11 Castle that can be easily moved
12 Hydroxyl-carbon compound
13 Fake out, on the rink
21 Electric guitar pioneer Paul
23 Chicken-king divider
25 Some are bookmarked
26 "Copy that"
27 Sporting wings
28 How Swayze once danced on film

29 Anklebone
30 Nixon's secretary
    of defense
31 First name in
    swashbucklers
32 Elizabeth II, to
    Edward VIII
34 A famous McCartney
37 "The Fly"
43 Pole with a blade
44 False front
45 Of the same sort
47 Leporid mammals
48 Big name in wrestling?

49 One still not
    clean after bathing
50 Verbal elbow
    in the ribs
51 Computer
    program errors
52 "Summertime,"
    in "Porgy and Bess," e.g.
53 Custom auto
    accessories
54 Not exactly a
    great depression
57 Football coaching
    legend Parseghian

SET THE TABLE

ACROSS

1 Whimpers
6 Take it easy
10 "Deck the Halls" syllables
14 "Farewell, François"
15 Soft spread
16 NYSE rival
17 Irish export
18 Certain championship event
20 "___ A Beautiful Morning"
21 Economize
23 Spooky
24 Oft-kicked item
25 Perpetual
27 Mirror, of yore
31 Making eyes at
32 Fix, as prices
33 Put to the test
36 Crinkled cotton fabric
37 It shoots the breeze
38 In a foul mood
40 It may be tapped
41 Jackie's second
42 Religious pilgrim
43 Site for a state slogan, perhaps
46 Books that may display where and tear?
49 Maui music makers
50 Hackneyed
51 Crossed one's fingers
53 GPs

56 Yellow flower
58 Net letter
60 Need liniment
61 Ives of song
62 Work on a pumpkin, perhaps
63 Pebble Beach pegs
64 ___-bitsy
65 Manipulate dough

DOWN

1 African republic
2 Abridge, maybe
3 First number in season records
4 Remick or Strasberg
5 Hawaii draw
6 Type of proposition
7 Styptic material
8 Dirigible balloon
9 Classified ad letters
10 Mailing supply
11 Love in Milan
12 Author Sinclair
13 Rods on rigs
19 Warren Beatty flick
22 Word with crab or cobra
24 CD player's malfunction
26 Faultfinder
27 It may be picked
28 Storybook monster
29 Cassini of fashion
30 Type of alcohol

33 Plebe's sch.
34 Annotation in proofreading
35 Bronte governess
37 Like some flowers
38 Stereo accessory
39 Building additions
41 Crackerjack
42 Lap dog, for short
43 Some coffeehouse orders
44 "That makes sense"

45 Furnish
46 Trip to the plate
47 Break in hostilities
48 Supple
52 Possessive pronoun
53 She ain't what she used to be
54 Opera star
55 Cold weather transport
57 Box score stat
59 Isle of ___

HERE'S A TOAST

ACROSS

1 Pincushion alternative
5 Rajiv Gandhi's grandfather
10 A little open
14 Former German capital
15 In great haste, at sea
16 Drawn fish
17 Love-in-a-mist bouquet
19 Hit the ground
20 Lounging locale
21 Love of life
22 Club that sings
23 Smoke detector
25 Off the beaten track
27 Veto
30 Cast of characters?
34 Stat that's good when low
35 Songstress Lena
37 End, in the Bible
38 Word with base or summer
40 It's removed by a stripper
42 Cutty ___ (historic ship)
43 Sure-footed creatures
45 "The Love Boat" employee
47 Old name preceder
48 Security feature
50 Cockscombs
52 Child's reward, perhaps
53 Proper word, at times
54 Tableland
56 Muse of history
59 Humidified
63 Czech runner Zatopek
64 Term of endearment
66 Without self-control
67 Massey of old movies
68 You can stick with it?
69 Turns into leather
70 Fine and ___
71 Powerful emotion

DOWN

1 Goes back to sea?
2 Track tipster
3 "___ Thee Oh Lord"
4 Vocalize, à la James Earl Jones
5 Veep under G.R.F.
6 One who runs the show
7 Heist tally
8 Regis sidekick Kelly
9 Open, as a change purse
10 Word games
11 Reagan's love
12 Tahiti sweetie
13 Memorization method
18 Historic time
24 Telegram punctuation
26 One of the five W's
27 Go over again
28 Do blackboard duty
29 Impromptu jazz performance

30 Cookie flavoring
31 Horne of "Stormy Weather" fame
32 Plume's source
33 Confiscates
36 Guard on the deck
39 Morale builders
41 Sandwich with a crunch
44 Doo-wop syllable
46 Morsel
49 Greenhouse plant

51 "Stop it!"
53 ". . . with ___ in sight"
54 Food group
55 1993 Oscar winner Thompson
57 Singer Falana
58 Barge ___ (interrupt)
60 "To Live and Die ___" (1985)
61 Bunny tail
62 "Of ___ I sing"
65 "Yippee!"

NOW YOU'RE COOKING

ACROSS

1 A Barrymore
6 Takes the bull by the horns
10 Portent
14 Campbell or Judd
15 Fingerboard ridge
16 Hemingway, for one
17 Bubbling, in a way
18 Memorization by repetition
19 Canyonlands locale
20 Home cook's low-cal staple?
23 Type of hold
24 It often comes to a stop
25 A guy on the green
26 Landmark Supreme Court name
29 Home cook's salad choice?
33 Albanian coin
34 Join forces, in a way
35 Chihuahua snack
36 Revise
39 Word with cap or coat
40 Country on the Irish Sea
41 TV's Roseanne
42 Honorarium
43 Tropical garland
44 Home cook's entree?
48 Title in India
49 Ward workers
50 Peachy keen
51 Historical period

54 Home cook's breakfast enhancement brand?
58 School visitor of rhyme
60 White wader
61 Aspirin targets
62 Jim Davis mutt
63 German actress Sommer
64 Tune for the unhip
65 Candlelike
66 Core element?
67 New drivers, often

DOWN

1 Put on the books
2 A profane state
3 Displeased audience member
4 Broadcast
5 Sadie Hawkins Day originator
6 From the top
7 Gator cousin
8 On a short leash
9 Braced (oneself)
10 Numbered piece
11 Kind of witness
12 Fed. regulator since 1970
13 "Ixnay"
21 Thick, messy stuff
22 Double switchback
27 Without repetition
28 Things that may become bruised

30 Trouble indicator
31 Nerdish guy
32 Prepare a slide
36 How-to stuff
37 Co-star of a
1939 classic
38 Backpacker's fare
39 Fit for repeated
service
40 Achilles' heel
42 Likes
43 Role for 37-Down

45 Work or energy unit
46 Upped the ante
47 Make fun of
52 Argument
53 Nave endings
55 Mind
56 "Easy Rider"
vehicle
57 Common ground
for Bush and Kerry
58 Contemptible
59 Decay-fighting org.

COLORFUL CLASSIC

ACROSS

1 Make meek, in a way
6 Totally bungled
10 It may be served in spots
13 Computer image element
14 Certain Asian royal
15 General assembly?
16 Frozen quarters
17 Comparable
18 "Mexican Spitfire" star Velez
19 Character in 36-Across
22 River's path, possibly
23 Haggard classic
24 Post-accident comment
26 Natural necklace
27 "The Sweater Girl" Turner
29 Fresno-to-Los Angeles dir.
30 Fed. stipend
32 Gladly, archaically
34 Understood
36 Classic film of 1939
39 "Sleuth" star
40 Bouquet
41 Copy
42 Ode subject
43 Many Little League coaches
45 Bay State cape
47 They're in red
49 Word with faced or fisted
50 Music form
53 Characters in 36-Across
57 Transgression
58 Certain allergic reaction
59 Epic tales
60 "The Virginian" author Wister
61 Butter alternative
62 Skating feats
63 IV installers
64 Miffed
65 Spine line

DOWN

1 Vengeful feeling
2 Euphoric states, slangily
3 Assembly line supply
4 Animal sound
5 Ava's role in "Mogambo"
6 Good thing to do for animals
7 Superior, for one
8 "National Velvet" author Bagnold
9 Excellent situation
10 Where you may get gas before eating
11 Put in italics
12 What the pros say
15 Choral part
20 Five-alarm item

21 Adult insect
25 Nevertheless
26 Lender's security
27 Clues, to a detective
28 Start for American
30 Defeat with a look
31 Tibias
33 Name on a shirt
35 In the blink ___ eye
37 United with
38 Quartered companion
39 Jersey chew

44 Nolan Ryan's team, once
46 Greets, in a way
48 Element number 26
49 Resort lake
50 Thesaurus compiler
51 In the least
52 Ad hoc oater group
54 Seraphic headdress
55 Strategic WWI river
56 Vehicle at a stand
57 Hide-hair link

GO FAR

ACROSS
1 "Still mooing," at a steakhouse
5 Spoil
10 Field measure
14 En route to England, in a way
15 It could be stuffed
16 Sweet-talk
17 Returning traveler's words
20 Swerves
21 In ___ (as found)
22 Word with parking or odd
23 Came into view
25 It increases one's chances of growth?
27 Dear old fellow
28 Short haircut
30 More sunburnt
31 Old salt
34 Shrews
35 "Start talkin'!"
37 Reach the breaking point
38 Rubbernecks
39 With "Way," an ancient Roman road
41 Jeanne d'Arc, e.g.
42 Norwegian rug
45 Isn't required to
47 Steak and lobster, e.g.
50 Entertainment system component
51 Clarinet's kin
53 Some casual wear
54 1958 hit song
57 Scientology founder Hubbard
58 "Family Ties" mother
59 Mideast gulf
60 Fax machine button
61 Harvests
62 Lease subject

DOWN
1 Embossed
2 Bronchial allergy
3 Plant anew
4 In the beaver state?
5 Labrador air base
6 Faithful or reliable word
7 They're at their best when boring
8 French 101 verb
9 One in the red
10 German interjection
11 Harding's successor
12 "End of the Century" rockers
13 Devonshire city
18 Alternative to .com or .net
19 Wife of Napoleon III
24 Long-gone birds
26 Washington follower
29 Contests in the ring
31 Serious

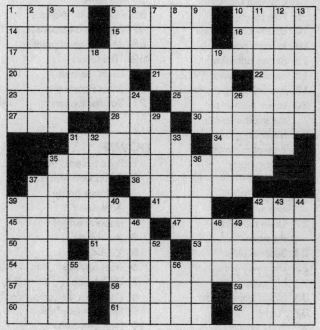

32 Talk of Toledo
33 Shred, as cheese
35 Live
36 Soaks
37 Greenwich ghost
39 Smithies' blocks
40 More high-minded
42 Put a new handle on?
43 Naval petty officer
44 Green light
46 Sheer fabric

48 First word of many a title
49 Extreme severity
52 "Watermark" chanteuse
55 Common connector
56 Recipe amt.

AFTER THE NEWS

ACROSS

1 Cordelia's father
5 Pale-faced
10 Lasses' companions
14 In times past
15 Strong adhesive
16 Snack item since 1912
17 Two following the news
20 Lower portion of the small intestine
21 Middling grade
22 Type of common denominator
23 Descend
25 College sr.'s exam, perhaps
27 Three following the news
34 Become older
35 Did away with, biblically
36 Naval base builder
37 Purges
39 Body pouch
41 Min. fractions
42 Go by, as time
45 Blackjack dealer's device
48 Word with down or key
49 Two following the news
52 What a tartan symbolizes
53 Goddess of the earth
54 Diarist Nin
57 Matter of law
59 Spanish resort island

63 Three following the news
66 Douglas or Wallace
67 Come to a consensus
68 At the highest point
69 "The Good Earth" heroine
70 Stiller's partner
71 Dundee toppers

DOWN

1 Point systems, in math
2 Compound with a hydroxyl group
3 Adolescent embarrassment
4 Just say no
5 ___ Lingus
6 Trout features
7 Use a strop
8 Outshines the competition
9 "Science Guy" Bill
10 Lynn and Swit
11 Leontyne Price piece
12 "Disco Duck" singer
13 Like an infielder's hands, supposedly
18 Sultans' associates
19 Nonchalant
24 Ravens org.
26 Librarian's utterances
27 Apple gadget
28 Like a good gymnast
29 Bicycle feature
30 Partly submerged

31 Ancient critical printing marks
32 Scout's mission, for short
33 "___ Have No Bananas"
38 Dissected frog, perhaps
40 More lame, as a joke
43 Chips go-with
44 Spaniard's "that"
46 Dinghy adjunct
47 Rocker Money

50 Send into a tizzy
51 Many a maze runner
54 BBs and .22s, e.g.
55 It may be acrylic
56 "Eso Beso (That Kiss!)" singer
58 II Chronicles follower
60 Least little bit
61 Camera feature
62 Roadie's burden
64 Leg, slangily
65 Teacher's org.

WATERCRAFT

ACROSS

1 New York Philharmonic conductor, 1978–91
6 Snatch
10 Sign of spring
14 '06 or '07, e.g.
15 Stop snoozing
16 Harvard rival
17 Start too soon
19 Latvia's capital
20 "How Sleep the Brave," for one
21 Polish
22 Hot
24 Hotel employee
26 Rectangle's four
27 Canal site
28 Corbin's "L.A. Law" role
29 Word that can follow the last word of 17- and 61-Across and 10- and 25-Down
32 "Cannery Row" character
34 Silas Marner's child
38 Gridlock components
40 When Thanksgiving is celebrated in Can.
41 Flies high
42 Not the final copy
43 Snores, comics-style
45 "___ in Cincinnati"
46 Made out
48 Nuptial or natal starter
50 Pulverized
53 Duke, marquis, earl, etc.
57 Divulge a secret
58 Indianapolis athlete
59 Tennis shot
60 Lot of land
61 Magazine for parents
64 Ostrich relative
65 Wraps up
66 Maverick's game
67 ". . . not always what they ___"
68 Out of the ordinary
69 Wield, as influence

DOWN

1 Low-pay position, in slang
2 Get away from
3 "Hill Street Blues" actress
4 1/6 oz.
5 Breathing problem
6 Edmund of "Miracle on 34th Street"
7 Infuriation
8 Half a Heyerdahl title
9 Robert Guillaume sitcom
10 "The Razor's Edge" star
11 Selassie of Ethopia
12 Rags-to-riches author
13 Withdraws gradually
18 Stockpile
23 Takes a stab at
25 Celebrate, in a way
26 Wholesale quantity, often

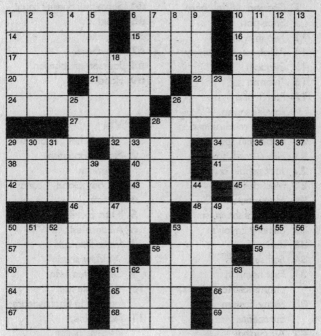

28 Rainbowlike
29 Like Leroy Brown
30 Lord's Prayer opener
31 One-time bridge
33 Seeped
35 Se Ri of the LPGA
36 Discount tag abbreviation
37 Clairvoyant's claim
39 Lesley of "60 Minutes"
44 Brief period
47 Pot, in the past

49 How to confirm a password
50 Celestial bodies
51 Papier-___ (art material)
52 "___ Grows in Brooklyn"
53 Grace under pressure
54 Similar
55 Office errand-boy
56 Movie critic Roger
58 USN officer
62 Collection of stories
63 Brine-cured salmon

FINAL SAY

ACROSS

1 Genoan official, once
5 Shoe part
11 Two in a billion?
14 Albatross, figuratively
15 Eyetooth
16 "Norma ___"
17 Part 1 of a solver's truism
19 Certain road runner
20 Cube with spots
21 Pick a card, say
22 Jack rabbit, actually
23 Most definite
26 Moon feature
28 Part 2 of the truism
32 Slithery Egyptian
33 Run
34 Sail supports
37 First name in pharmaceutical giants
38 Many Eastern Europeans
42 Air current heading skyward
45 Start for colonial
46 Part 3 of the truism
51 Renaissance rulers of Florence
52 Basic knitting stitches
53 Hippies' quarters
54 Halloween persona
57 Populous city area, slangily
58 Jack Horner's last words
59 End of the truism
64 Serve that doesn't count
65 Scold
66 ___ fixe
67 Whichever
68 Jackson or Johnson
69 Hoodwinks

DOWN

1 "How is he?" addressee
2 Noted Japanese-American
3 "Goody Goody" candy
4 Detects
5 It has a chilling effect
6 Alliance est. in 1949
7 Make little cuts
8 Window shade?
9 Celebrated twin
10 Vegetable that features in Shakespeare
11 Margarine, vis-à-vis butter
12 Hardy companion?
13 Weather person's adjective
18 Of reduced degree
22 Shirley Booth role
23 Dupe's undoing
24 Star bear
25 Number for the show
26 IRS calculator?
27 Tiresome routines
29 "Lulu" or "Norma"
30 Switching device

31 Go with the flow
35 Capital of Tunisia
36 Done on ___ (without contract)
39 Disease-fighting protein
40 Shrimp discard
41 Part of Buck's trilogy
43 Motorist's crime, briefly
44 Give it a whirl; it's fun!
46 High-jumping antelope
47 Mariners

48 Three-legged calf, for one
49 Oversupply
50 Caterpillar-eating insect
54 It can be rounded up
55 Winged
56 Prize fight's take
59 Not yet decided, on a sched.
60 She lies around the farm
61 Use a Singer
62 Bodybuilder's unit
63 ___ Plaines, Illinois

YOUR DEAL

ACROSS

1 Hawthorne's "Mosses From an Old ___"
6 Five partner
10 What thsi is
14 Admits bluntly
15 Irani currency
16 Achilles' weak point
17 Performance-based pay increase
19 To be, in old Rome
20 Quarter-deck?
21 "A ___ a Kill" (Bond film)
23 Boo-boo
26 Neeson of "Schindler's List"
28 Double twist
29 Cleveland-to-Pittsburgh dir.
30 Deft storyteller
33 Cash partner
35 Corporation emblem
36 Appear to be
39 Spelunker's site
40 This puzzle's theme
41 Emulate Lucky Lindy
42 Amino, for one
43 Alamo competitor
44 Adrien of cosmetics
45 On cloud nine
48 Wrap up
49 Wrath
51 Arctic Ocean obstacle
52 Aphrodite's love
54 Drink of the gods
56 Legendary newsman Sevareid
57 Ruler in Rimsky-Korsakov operas
58 Word processing process
64 Provoke
65 Removes a squeak from
66 "Velvet Fog" vocalist
67 Word of exclusivity
68 Zap
69 Koufax of baseball fame

DOWN

1 Type of Mayan
2 Hail from the past
3 ". . . borrower ___ a lender be"
4 Sound of a perfect jump shot
5 Inlet
6 Mild euphemism
7 "Rocky ___"
8 Barker and Rainey
9 Way to get to the top, perhaps
10 ". . . 'tis of ___"
11 Store window sign
12 Royal pains
13 Some corn-oil products
18 Gifford's successor
22 "___ Mine" (Beatles song)
23 Hajj destination

Puzzle 80

24 Sci-fi writer Asimov
25 Repairman's visit
26 Seeking dates
27 Swallow
31 Shamrock
32 Cold War letters
34 Give a makeover
37 Nicholas Gage heroine
38 Casting equipment
40 Passaic River city
44 Chocoholics, e.g.
46 Jazz gp.

47 Scruggs of bluegrass
49 Musician's lead-in
50 Violinist's accessory
53 Nobelist Severo ___
55 Small card
56 Ultimatum's ultimate word, usually
59 More, musically
60 Antlered creature
61 Fish-eating coastal bird
62 Mil. officer's position
63 CTRL, e.g.

STAY SHARP!

ACROSS

1 The end of ___
6 Provoke
11 Second Amendment rights org.
14 "L'Enfer" poet Clément
15 Mock
16 "Dig in!"
17 It's used in dimly lit conditions
19 Tokyo, formerly
20 Country singer Kathy
21 Word with honey or spelling
22 Norse god
23 Mortgage consideration
25 Actress Wood
27 Circus impresario
31 Perform high-tech surgery
32 Communal word
33 Storied plantation?
34 Blink of an eye
37 Stuffed shirt
39 First word follower of 17- and 64-Across and 11- and 29-Down
42 Father
43 Two-masted vessels
45 Within earshot
47 D.C. VIP
48 Get but good

50 Tangles
52 Beehive and bouffant
55 Overhang
56 It has a blunt end
57 Shaggy beast
59 Bequeaths
63 LP speed
64 Employ a woodworking technique
66 551, in stone
67 Doo-wop favorite, e.g.
68 Fiji neighbor
69 Application check box
70 Ralph of "The Waltons"
71 Sound like a bull

DOWN

1 Dial choices
2 "The Lion King" lion
3 "Was to be," in Latin
4 Platforms for speakers
5 Deep down
6 K-12 group
7 Poetic foot
8 Chess piece
9 Imaginary
10 Greek letter
11 Gar
12 Spokes
13 Send a note of apology, e.g.
18 Snooze
22 Desert refuge
24 Mark successor

26 Muslim cap
27 Floral arrangement
28 Salad type
29 Betty Crocker product
30 Neighbor of Quebec
35 Complimentary
36 Longings
38 Strident sound
40 Hawaiian goose
41 Tex-Mex snack
44 Caesar's first name
46 Goes back

49 Chicago university
51 Add flavor to
52 Zebra groups
53 Jobs site?
54 Mecca resident
58 Make a sweater
60 Chianti, e.g.
61 MIT grad, maybe
62 Bridge relative
64 Container of
    fresh milk
65 Ball prop

MATERIAL THINGS

ACROSS

1 Killarney and Lomond
6 Heavenly sight
10 Building projection
14 Everglades resident
15 Wall covering, perhaps
16 Shredded side
17 "Gladiator" setting
18 Sniggler's haul
19 Brobdingnagian
20 Vim and vigor
21 Gap-toothed actor
24 Escape the clutches of
26 "___ American Cousin"
27 Unit named for a French physicist
29 Rectifies
34 Halt
35 Midshipman's counterpart
36 "Butterflies ___ Free"
37 Performs musically, in a way
38 Measure of dignity
39 Cornell's ___ Hall
40 Ox attachment
41 Fake name
42 Split
43 Dilapidated
45 Bother continually
46 Suffix with Darwin
47 Some candy containers

48 Water moccasin
53 Restriction
56 Deseret, now
57 Ages upon ages
58 Type of orange
60 Less or some preceder
61 Hairline cut
62 Happen again
63 Cicatrix
64 Sound stages
65 Word with truth or ambition

DOWN

1 "Able to ___ tall buildings . . ."
2 Fairy tale heavy
3 Party decoration
4 Pullet's elder
5 Eminence
6 One cubic meter
7 Tower part
8 Treaty signer
9 Brought back to original condition
10 Having missed the boat
11 Horner's discovery
12 Heroic chronicle
13 Rams' mates
22 City near Arnhem
23 On the disabled list
25 Sale-priced
27 Having a sharp taste
28 Opponent of Lee

29 Jeweler's unit
30 Poems of tribute
31 North American
wild duck
32 Apple and pear
33 Crystal ball users, e.g.
35 "Blondie" creator
Young
38 Property of an
attractively thin person
39 Dried-up
41 Furthermore

42 Cornet kin
44 Any one of the two
45 Stolen, slangily
47 Some mantel pieces
48 Skips class
49 Concerning the ear
50 Scarlett's place
51 Burrowing creature
52 "Put a lid ___!"
54 A malarial fever
55 Eggheady sort
59 Mermaid's home

MIDDLE VOWELS

ACROSS
1 Gruff-sounding
7 Quahog, e.g.
11 Bacillus shape
14 As originally placed
15 Places
16 Wax trapper
17 Effervescent Dr.
18 New Year's word
19 Four-stringed instrument, for short
20 Doc wannabes
23 Tadpole cousins
27 Valentine's Day offering
28 Pumas' pads
29 Sour grapes?
31 Seat for two or more
32 Gain access
33 Nullify
36 Always, in verse
37 In the thick of things
40 Test starter
43 Polyphonic song
44 Old photo tint
48 Go back
50 Thoroughly
52 Rousseau novel
53 Draped dress
55 Little one
56 Garb for the jet set
59 "___ Gotta Be Me"
60 Walk with weariness
61 Make-believe food
66 Fractional monetary unit of Japan
67 Water drainer
68 Krauss of bluegrass
69 Time of the 75th meridian
70 Cultivated grasses
71 Christening activity

DOWN
1 Kind of roof
2 Next to nothing?
3 "Little Orphan Annie" character
4 Famous oversleeper
5 Bloom support
6 Archimedes' cry
7 '03 or '04, e.g.
8 Oafs
9 Nonprofit org. since 1920
10 Global hot spot
11 Get back together
12 Yellow ribbon bearer
13 Armoire kin
21 Most urgent
22 Nosh
23 Time before anything
24 Radiator part
25 It does blowups
26 Look
30 Scythe-bearing visitor
31 Belgrade-to-Athens dir.
34 AAA suggestion
35 Conductor Toscanini
38 Hi and Lois' kid
39 Satisfy, as demands

Puzzle 83

40 Assumption
41 Withdraws
42 Clear
45 Snoop
46 Kind
47 Supporter's response
49 Folklore being
51 Jack Haley role
53 What push comes to
54 Executive's staff
57 Leave helpless
  with laughter

58 Toni Morrison novel
62 Not very bright, really
63 Chi-omega
  connection
64 It's never neutral
65 Noted twin

SHAPE UP

ACROSS
1 "Cool it!" Italian style
6 Les ___-Unis
11 Handle moguls?
14 Room at the top
15 Poisonous
16 Blood, so to speak
17 Star transport
19 Pointy-eared sprite
20 Protective case
21 Gray wolf
22 Court
23 Churchyard tree in "Romeo and Juliet"
24 Bunch of moola
26 Rock genre
28 Prepares an apple, perhaps
30 It has a blind spot
33 Major League manager Larry
36 Uses a shuttle
38 Word with blood or organ
39 Sixth day creation
40 Iron output
42 Chance upon
43 Stable fathers
45 Juno, to the Greeks
46 Man, but not woman
47 Repressed
49 Cousin of lavender
51 Sinful city
53 Don't just stand there
54 Doe or heifer, e.g.
57 Reheat, nowadays

59 Peter Gunn's girlfriend
61 Farmer, essentially
63 Woolly mama
64 Talk and talk and talk
66 School of tomorrow?
67 Have pizza delivered
68 Toil
69 Word with hat or hand
70 "___ Remember" (1960 song)
71 Lugged

DOWN
1 Too heavy on the low notes
2 "___ Hop" ('50's hit)
3 Scatter, as seeds
4 "___ yellow ribbon . . ."
5 When Romeo says "Juliet is the sun"
6 Biblical or ordinal suffix
7 Car payment
8 Self-evident principle
9 Woodcutter's cry
10 Went hastily
11 They never intersect in geometry
12 Pusher's purchase, perhaps
13 Facts, briefly
18 Maps out
25 One of Franklin's two certainties

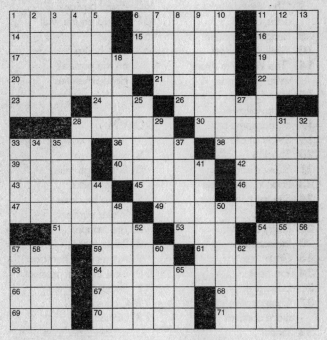

27 Type of power or clock
28 Regained consciousness
29 Pittsburgh product
31 Holiday song
32 Jocular Johnson
33 Enjoy the limelight
34 Jon Arbuckle's pooch
35 Sci-fi travel term
37 Delhi wraps
41 Bad-mouth
44 Extra wager

48 Affectionate denial
50 Idle
52 Like many a mouthwash
54 It pours from pores
55 Laborious throw
56 Committed a faux pas
57 Round number
58 MP's concern
60 Better copy
62 Capital on a fjord
65 Beatle bride

VIPS

ACROSS

1 "The Wolf Man" actor Lugosi
5 Hedge component
10 Walk with effort
14 "The Way We Were" writer Bergman
15 Monopoly purchase
16 Theta follower
17 Burdensome boss
19 Stride at a track
20 Shackle
21 Show clearly
23 Prior to, in poems
24 Site for tying knots
26 "G'day, ___!"
28 Postgrad deg.
29 Indisposed
33 Garb
34 Top boss
36 Eden exile
37 Comparatively more comical
38 Tenth anniversary gift
39 Chief plotter
41 Court defense
42 Montreal's railway
43 Trig. function
44 Roll call response
45 Rockies resort
47 Sword conqueror
48 Black Sea locale
51 Heart part
55 Paper starter
56 Oppressive boss
59 Church recess
60 Postal device
61 Put up on the wall
62 Pb
63 Little house on the prairie?
64 Hotel amenities

DOWN

1 Take the point off a foil
2 Joie de vivre
3 Edinburgh miss
4 Bobbysocks
5 It can be close
6 Water carrier
7 Tire trapper
8 Put to work
9 Artist's cap, perhaps
10 Blast furnace product
11 Shark's offer
12 Of the ear
13 Dinner and a movie, perhaps
18 Stable mom
22 Reason for a decoration
24 Leave in the lurch
25 Word on a certain door
26 Hollywood release
27 Actor's representative
28 Dennis of comics, for one
30 Paul Newman, for one

31 Your of yore
32 Use a whetstone
33 Presidential run
34 Peach or plum
35 That girl
37 Dentist's suggestion
40 Comprehended
41 Pinnacles
44 Damsel's deliverer
46 Name in brewing
47 Blender setting
48 Fiery gem

49 Gullible one
50 She was born free
51 Skilled
52 Fellow
53 Headey or Horne
54 Work units
57 What a game
may break
58 Extraction's creation

REAL MOTION PICTURES

ACROSS

1 Isn't supporting
6 Presidential campaign subject
10 Video snippet
14 Dead, as an engine
15 Partner of aid
16 Word with strike or school
17 State or national starter
18 Force-ful teacher?
19 Film canine
20 TRAIN film
23 Hinny's kin
26 "The Gold Bug" writer
27 Palindromic exclamation
28 White House nickname
29 Plenty of bread
31 Word with T or dry
33 Made a choice
35 Archimedes' cry
37 Gratify
39 PLANE movie (with "The")
44 Native Alaskan
45 Muppets creator
46 Pin the blame on
49 Daly of "Judging Amy"
51 Korean border river
52 "___ Not Unusual" (Tom Jones hit)
53 Denouement

55 "Double Fantasy" artist
57 "When We Was ___" (Harrison tune)
58 AUTOMOBILE movie
62 Ran like heck
63 Democritus' unit
64 Chocolate-yielding tree
68 Send forth
69 More than mega-
70 Loan shark's offense
71 Pirates' rivals
72 Valkyries' master
73 Union foe

DOWN

1 Compete in the combined
2 "The Hundred Secret Senses" author
3 Quick, as a study
4 Bemoans
5 "Doonesbury" or "Dilbert"
6 Lower level team
7 One of the reeds
8 Cowpunchers' gear
9 Squirrel away
10 Industrial mogul
11 Go ballistic
12 Consumption
13 Somewhat ill
21 Track down
22 Flute sound
23 Pub potables
24 Beginning course, often

25 Indira's dress
30 Wild
32 Koufax, notably
34 Indiana's state flower
36 Out of ___ (awry)
38 Goddess of wisdom
40 Not in vogue
41 Letters on a jet
42 Thelma Harper's neighbor
43 Cold-shoulder
46 More qualified

47 Where charity begins?
48 Log-on name
50 Bates of "Psycho"
54 "Swell!"
56 Take place
59 Understands
60 Moldings at the bases of columns
61 Lighten, as a burden
65 Novice reporter
66 What may follow you
67 Olive with a little salt?

GOOD ADVICE

ACROSS

1 "Absolute Torch and Twang" singer
5 Oblong tomato variety
9 A, B, and O pertaining to blood
14 Appian Way, e.g.
15 "The Wizard ___"
16 Chanteuse Lena
17 Quip, Part 1
20 Montana, for one
21 "Told you so!"
22 Hardly old-fashioned
23 Quip, Part 2
29 Legendary siren
30 Hand for Snoopy?
31 Form 1040 org.
32 Astronomer Carl
35 Eliot's miser Marner
39 To ___ (exactly)
41 "The Rehearsal" impressionist painter
43 Kind of call
44 Israeli Moshe
46 City on the Seine
48 Word with water or jet
49 Funny Caesar
51 Responded to
53 Quip, Part 3
58 Turner or Cole
59 Wiley Post's monoplane, The Winnie ___
60 Kennel sound
61 Quip's end
68 It comes from the heart
69 Sweet edible fruit
70 Pinochle declaration
71 One way to remove tough floor stains, perhaps
72 Urban hazard
73 B'way success signs

DOWN

1 "Chinatown Family" author Yutang
2 ___ Z (you name it)
3 One of the original 13 colonies
4 Stylus target
5 Cone's retinal partner
6 Frequently, to poets
7 Large ruminant
8 Central Mexican civilization, once
9 Article everyone's familiar with
10 Exclamation of pain
11 Word with donna or ballerina
12 "Entry of Christ Into Brussels" artist
13 Run-down
18 Lively dances
19 Uriah of "David Copperfield"
23 Homer's epic poem
24 Kind of, in slang
25 Prove your literacy
26 Its capital is Niamey
27 Airline created in 1946
28 Do the butterfly
33 Long trailer?
34 Eight-square-mile republic in the Pacific

36 Words preceding "Take it or leave it"
37 "American Idol" runner-up
38 Playground equipment
40 Word with Near or Far
42 Ooze
45 Federal medical agcy.
47 River nymph
50 Moore of the movies
52 Floppy disk successors
53 George Washington: "First ___, first . . ."

54 Nevada resort site
55 Nor'easter, e.g.
56 Smooths wood
57 Too early for lunch
62 "How was ___ know?"
63 Gullible one
64 Ike's command in WWII
65 Brain wave reading (Abbr.)
66 UN workers' grp.
67 Gridiron stats

STRANGE ZOO

ACROSS

1 Hunting target
5 Word on terrycloth, sometimes
8 King and queen, e.g.
14 A combining form meaning "air"
15 Giant great
16 Highway access
17 Accident-probing org.
18 Debussy's "La ___"
19 One-named folk singer
20 NASCAR pit worker, e.g.
23 Bicycle built for two
24 Dole (out)
25 Brave moguls
28 "___ to Psyche"
29 Break fast or breakfast
31 Mimic
33 Half of an audio cassette
35 Hearing aids
36 It could be found in the attic
41 Long, long time
42 Regions
43 Super saver?
47 Pt. of USDA
48 Public transport
51 Mork's planet
52 They sometimes clash
54 Note in the A major scale
56 Result of a rough workout, perhaps
58 Pancake simile
61 Olive, for one
62 Elisabeth of "Leaving Las Vegas"
63 Sound at an opened floodgate
64 "Just the Way You ___"
65 Informed
66 Noted Kitt
67 Born
68 Fix, at the vet's office

DOWN

1 Serenaded
2 Any foursome
3 First name in detective fiction
4 Turn
5 Like Mom's apple pie
6 List unit
7 Senator Thurmond
8 Grew fond of
9 Financially strapped
10 Deuce beater
11 Back muscle, to Billy Blanks
12 CPR giver
13 Relaxing resort
21 "Now you ___, now . . ."
22 Compaq rival
25 Sweep with binoculars
26 Go-___ (small racer)
27 "___ Now Or Never"
30 Driver's aid

32 Pro votes
33 Trap topper
34 Chicken ___ king
36 Tear's partner
37 Pawn
38 Big Band ___
39 "Fever" singer
40 Like some criticism
41 GI's address
44 Go over and over and . . .
45 Mystery writer Christie
46 Craggy height
48 Cruise the pubs
49 Actress Andress
50 Rapid
53 "Wake of the Ferry" painter
55 Party givers
56 Coagulate
57 Land of the leprechaun
58 Wonderment
59 ___ Na Na
60 Word with "openers"

GO FOR A SPIN

ACROSS

1 In the same place, in a bibliog.
5 Divine Bette
10 Room off an ambulatory
14 Nasty comments
15 Communion site
16 Diez x diez
17 Handel's "Hercules" heroine
18 Alternate tactic
19 "When I Was ___" ("HMS Pinafore" song)
20 Space-saving steps?
23 "___ Doppelgänger" (Theodor Storm work)
24 Mauna ___, Hawaii
25 Professional obi wearer
26 Film genre
28 Mouth, slangily
31 Provide food, uptown
32 What a joke may break
34 Giant, to Jack
36 Commuters' lines
37 Ringlet
42 Kind of artist
43 Notwithstanding, for short
44 "The Raven" monogram
45 ". . . ___ of meat from the king" (2 Samuel 11:8)
48 Proud-peacock link
50 Sunday song

54 Remedied a badly installed carpet
56 Common article
58 Lead-in for Bravo
59 Gyrating Muslim monk
63 Superlative
64 1988 Olympics setting
65 Just the facts?
66 Hook's sidekick
67 Yawning gap
68 From the start
69 Towel embroidery
70 Pimlico garb
71 Extract a tooth

DOWN

1 "White" and "scarlet" birds
2 "Ali," e.g.
3 Fighting Big Ten team
4 "In the headlights" animal
5 Syrup source
6 "You're darned right!"
7 At bats or runs, e.g.
8 Capital of Yemen
9 Character in gangster film spoofs
10 Spiny bush
11 Rectangular column
12 Beachcomber's find
13 Makes lovable
21 "I Get ___ Out of You" (Cole Porter)
22 Tape-player button
27 Christmas tree type

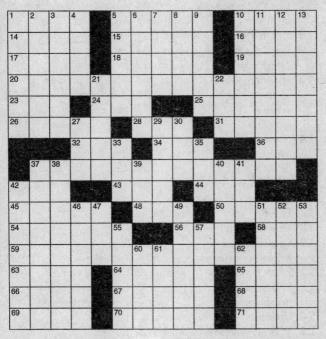

29 Jackson Five features
30 "The Tell-Tale Heart" author
33 Suffix in the Guinness book
35 Member of the flock
37 Plea to Lassie
38 Stand-up's staple
39 When repeated, a ballroom dance
40 Prank
41 FedEx alternative
42 Service station sideline
46 Calcutta clothing (Var.)
47 The "S" of RSVP
49 In the early evening
51 Richards of "Jurassic Park"
52 Lend an ear
53 Eye-catching haircut
55 Spinal column features
57 Wheels at sea
60 Radar's favorite pop
61 Aim
62 War's end

GONE TOO SOON

ACROSS

1 Bloc that dissolved in 1991
5 Full range
9 Responds à la "Jeopardy!"
13 "Sabrina, the Teenage Witch" actress Caroline
14 Show validity
15 Word with gift or thrift
16 "The Subject Was Roses" star Patricia
17 Realtors' units
18 Have feelings
19 One who had momentary success
22 Ethan Hawke, to Denzel Washington
24 Upturned
25 With 41-Across, description of a has-been
29 Kuwaiti leaders
30 Hamlet, for one
31 "Mystery!" channel
34 Neutral shades
35 Rock opera by the Who
37 Something to raise
38 Director Lee
39 Burt's wife, once
40 Body section
41 See 25-Across
44 Charter publications?
47 Ozzie and Harriet, e.g.
48 Terse
52 Working stiff
53 Pauline's problem
54 Ade flavor
57 Sea eagle
58 Ranks contestants
59 Organic compound
60 Swallow flat
61 Outer limit
62 Work-weary exclamation

DOWN

1 Mantel piece
2 Haggard work
3 Sailor's way of life
4 Come-from-behind teams
5 Curved
6 Spelling or Amos
7 It's within range
8 Gusto
9 Go to a higher level
10 Mold or fashion
11 Islamic text
12 Pass bills
14 Toyota model
20 Wee workers
21 Fine-tune
22 Eta's follower
23 Staff anew

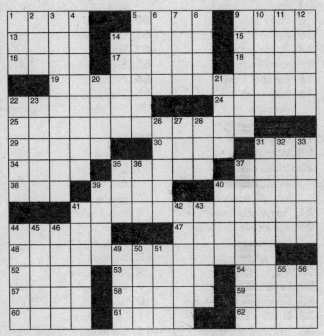

26 Word on a ticket
27 Orange food
28 Word with "takers"
31 Mindlessly repeating
32 Buffalo kin
33 Bamboozles
35 Cargo measure
36 The first cardinal
37 Breastplate
39 In need of a map
40 Metalware
41 January birthstone

42 Type of kick, in football
43 Whimpers
44 Vail rival
45 Yonder
46 Batty-sounding birds
49 Cathedral area
50 It can be pressing
51 Small amount
55 Miss Piggy's pronoun
56 Mischievous little creature

WHAT A GIANT SAYS

ACROSS

1 Rogue
6 Party type
10 Peaked
14 "I was out of town," e.g.
15 Head of France
16 Rodriguez behind the plate
17 200 milligrams
18 Suspicious of
19 Wither
20 "Send men to ___ out the land of Canaan"
21 Hollywood investment
24 Transforms cod into bacalao
25 747 kitchen
26 Ms. Lansbury
29 Be revolting?
30 Collector's ultimatum
33 Dallas inst.
36 Lawyer Dershowitz
37 Be under the weather
38 Famous septet
39 Soak
40 Impersonal mail
44 Treats hides
45 More cruel
46 Attack
49 Oriental
51 Gridiron goof
53 Russian fighter
56 Sweet sandwich
57 Bedouin
58 Gray's churchyard poem
60 Bring up
61 Urn
62 Fabulist
63 Slips up
64 Pitcher
65 They may be allayed

DOWN

1 Alveoli
2 Give it up, so to speak
3 Ethereal
4 Industrialist's deg.
5 Trap
6 Ermine
7 Big tops
8 Aleutian isle
9 Virgil work
10 Nonsense
11 Do the trick
12 Big dipper?
13 One on a Nixon list
22 Gung-ho spirit
23 Relaxation
24 Leo's son, the actor
26 Distant
27 Battle of the ___, 1798
28 Punkie
29 Lunar valley
31 Skiff propellers
32 Young Cratchit
33 Observed

34 Stable mom
35 Cold War concern
38 Getz on the sax
40 Pass alternative
41 Vacationing
42 Ludwig or Jannings
43 Shredded and bagged item
44 Small drums
46 In advance
47 More certain
48 Apply lipstick poorly
49 Humiliate
50 It has a duel purpose
52 Performer who fills the club
53 New Mexico silhouette
54 Inventor Sikorsky
55 Shortchanges
59 Lighthorse Harry

RATS!

ACROSS

1. ___ And Span (household cleanser)
5. Nutty
9. Monks' hoods
14. Cowboy Larue
15. Malarial fever
16. Enthusiastic cry
17. Eagle by the sea
18. Make the grade
19. Daycare lineup
20. Poolside threat
23. Program abbr.
24. Lilliputian
25. "One Flew Over the Cuckoo's Nest" writer
27. Working mom's helper
30. Wife of Abraham
31. Winningest lefty
32. Pass over
34. Marina feature
37. Site selection org.
38. Big cheese
41. Vessel with a pedestal
42. "Lonely Boy" singer
44. Pen points
45. Result
47. Sashay
49. Cinch
50. British honorees
51. Even bet
53. Tie the knot
54. 1991 news subject
59. Area measurement
61. Clue
62. Toledo's lake
63. It'll give you cold comfort
64. Garfield's pal
65. Festive
66. Like Inspector Clouseau
67. Marina feature
68. "Galveston" crooner Campbell

DOWN

1. Killed, in Judges
2. Troopers' head?
3. Proven otherwise
4. Fastest four-legger
5. Jaunty
6. Once more
7. Hard to please
8. Anxiety producer
9. Tour de France entrant
10. Sculler's gear
11. Landmark since John Adams' day
12. Influential group
13. Slugging superstar
21. Prepare for a second printing
22. Giraffe cousin
26. Bummed out
27. Home to most humans
28. Conversant with
29. Beast of burden's burden

30 Beverage samples
32 Fit of anger
33 One-time CIA target
35 Spanish actress Penelope
36 Word with bend or jerk
39 Currently occupied
40 The socially lost
43 S&L convenience
46 Fund for the future
48 Extremely popular

49 One making a sacrifice, maybe
50 Condescend
51 Shirley Temple role
52 Comical Kovacs
53 VE Day setting
55 Charcuterie, e.g.
56 Like some vaccines
57 Exasperate
58 Malicious
60 Word with hat or coat

LOW BRIDGE

ACROSS

1 Unquestioning, as faith
6 Door fastener
10 Window part
14 Half of an '80s crime-fighting duo
15 Capital on a fjord
16 "Beetle Bailey" pooch
17 Kind of zoo exhibit
18 "Passages" writer Sheehy
19 Lunchtime, for many
20 BRIDGE
23 Foot-pound subdivision
24 Million ___ March
25 Long hikes
26 Record producer's work
27 Heels
30 Cambridge sch.
31 '70s police drama
33 Sonata, e.g.
34 Repudiate
35 BRIDGE
38 Roy's partner
39 Doubt-conveying interjection
40 Rugrats
41 Addition
42 Checked out
43 "A Bridge Too ___"
44 Ski run
46 Tailor's need
47 Seek change?

50 BRIDGE
55 Triumphant cry
56 Skilled diver
57 Dubuque denizen
58 Put in the mail
59 Tapered tuck
60 How low can you go?
61 Energy bits
62 Tacks on
63 Fashion

DOWN

1 Barber's accessory
2 Rod, of the courts
3 "Happy Birthday" medium
4 Kind of little package
5 Nobel's invention
6 Links great Ben
7 "Hurry up," on memos
8 Word with pink or pillow
9 Campaigner's barometer
10 Submarine detector
11 Reconciliation
12 They get stuffed once per year
13 Candor
21 Careless
22 Where-at link
26 Perth pal
27 Like many hams
28 Teensy bit

29 Microsoft product
31 Performer with a sword
32 Hitting hard
33 Pang
34 Fashionable Christian
36 Bit of hope?
37 Pinch hitters
38 Abhor
42 Undulating fish
43 Christmas buy
45 Cedes the pigskin

46 Huffs and puffs
47 Like some limericks
48 It doesn't need a stamp
49 Romance or sci-fi, e.g.
51 "Same Time, Next Year" actor
52 Where you may find a fork
53 It may lead to an outlet
54 Feta source

STREAKERS

ACROSS

1 Bibliographic space saver
5 Crude dwellings
9 Celestial firework
14 Abnormal breathing
15 Brilliantly colored food fish
16 Worship
17 Flowering plant from South Africa
18 Burrowing insectivore
19 Leg bone
20 9-Across
23 Stolen, slangily
24 Anti-price-fixing agcy.
25 Cable channel
28 Physicist Niels
31 Old undergarment
36 "Coffee, Tea ___?"
38 Angora output
40 It was given statehood in 1820
41 9-Across
44 Milo or Tessie
45 Powerful shark
46 Some female parents
47 Like a cloudless night
49 Bart's sister
51 Corned beef holder
52 Gumshoe
54 Shade provider
56 9-Across
65 Vocally
66 Nondairy spread
67 Folk singer Mitchell
68 Crown
69 Barbecue offering, perhaps
70 Final notice, briefly
71 It's a crying need
72 British nobleman
73 Wagers

DOWN

1 Estrada of TV
2 Kind of dancer
3 Returned to the perch
4 "Lifestyles of the Rich and Famous" host
5 Everybody has one
6 Well briefed about
7 Baby powder ingredient
8 Rock ledge
9 Underground burial site
10 God of war and poetry
11 Unruly crowds
12 Pennsylvania county
13 Sign of sorrow
21 Fireplace ledge
22 Abbr. after a comma
25 Santa remarks
26 French seaport
27 Creighton University site
29 1947 Oscar winner Celeste

30 Part of RCMP
32 Event at Minsky's
33 Lute of India
34 Foe
35 Concise
37 Always
39 Norse god of discord
42 Environmentalists' celebration
43 Big game in college
48 Vote for
50 Chicken ___ king

53 Like some calls
55 Low-paying employment, slangily
56 Shower alternative
57 Pelvic bones
58 Shark's offering
59 Wait in hiding
60 Jazzy Fitzgerald
61 Planetary revolution
62 Honshu seaport
63 The "U" of CPU
64 Cherry parts

IN THE SADDLE

ACROSS

1 Alphabetic run
6 Greasy spoon fare
10 Image to click on
14 Fox drama
15 Spread in a tub
16 Basilica center
17 Certain carriage, or a really bad sketch of one
19 "Rag Mop" brothers
20 "Spoon River" poet's monogram
21 They have parental instincts
22 Proposals
24 Bring back
26 Run at the mouth
27 Have as a subsidiary
28 Checkers across the Atlantic
31 Wimps' opposites
34 Buck or Bailey
35 Alleged paranormalist Geller
36 Outback avians
37 Sentimental one
38 Industrial-strength air?
39 Need nursing
40 Church recesses
41 Perception factor
42 One with the shivers
44 Baltimore starter?
45 Mah-jongg equipment
46 Sugar servings
50 Head of a pen
52 He hit 66 homers in 1998
53 Miss Piggy's pronoun
54 "Good heavens!"
55 Nintendo's big hit in 1981
58 Billiard cushion
59 Clarinet cousin
60 Digested
61 Sea eagle
62 Some are prime
63 Color changers

DOWN

1 Preoperative delivery, once
2 Cello feature
3 Cold carriers?
4 Christmas Eve syllables
5 Take care of a pitcher's arm
6 Khan's Golden
7 Old-style "Bummer!"
8 Put in stitches
9 Like some degrees
10 Bewildered
11 Mound in the Sahara?
12 Kaput
13 Good or bad ending
18 Sock-mender's oath?
23 Court offense
25 Ten below?
26 Old-fashioned exclamations
28 Postpone an action

Puzzle 95

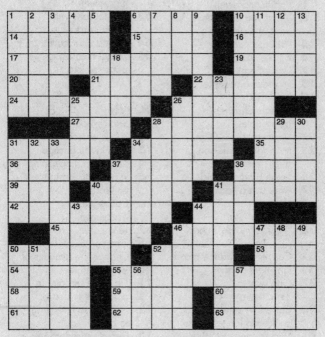

29 Race pace
30 Audible breath
31 Microwave
32 Arab potentate
33 Frankie Laine hit of 1949
34 Masquerades
37 Magnificence
38 Be "it"
40 Having the means
41 Rotted
43 Center
44 Statue part

46 Nudges
47 Be a drama queen
48 Photocopying need
49 Speaks without speaking
50 Word with "number one"
51 Lab medium
52 Downlooker
56 ___-Wan Kenobi
57 Diane in "The Godfather"

A STAR IS BORN

ACROSS

1 Fortification wall
8 What you may catch the gardener doing
15 Put on a pedestal
16 It goes "pssst!"
17 Uncle Sam's take
18 Provides a room for
19 Bolshevik
20 Signals Christie's appreciates
21 Medevac destinations
22 Marjorie Henderson Buell's moppet
26 Some bind, it's said
27 "Key Largo" actress Hagen
28 "Cocoon" star
30 "Animal House" tune, "___ Lama Ding Dong"
32 Catcher behind the plate?
33 First light of day
37 One way to get attention
40 Chocolate sandwich cookie no longer made
41 "Riddle-me-___!" ("Guess!")
42 Poi source
43 1 followed by 100 zeros
45 Hasty escape
46 Notable broccoli hater
49 Brad Pitt's sackful
53 Inc.'s kin
54 Sinatra hit, after "All"
55 Name in a landmark court case
56 Just for kicks
58 When on these runways, models move very quickly

62 Traditional pudding ingredient
63 Crustaceans with seven pairs of legs
64 Does a slow burn
65 Radon measuring package, e.g.

DOWN

1 Smallest part of MPH
2 Public order?
3 Gun in the garage
4 Keep from happening
5 Word with "instrument" or "control"
6 Conservatory assignment
7 To a ___
8 Free conditionally
9 Change the attitudes of
10 Vases with feet
11 "To be" alternate, in a famous soliloquy
12 Nipponese immigrant to U.S.
13 Dame's introduction
14 Superficial luster
20 What most fans think we are
22 First person you'll see when visiting "The Addams Family"
23 Home of the Sistine Chapel
24 Made the wild mild
25 "Had I ___ for a century dead" (Tennyson)
26 Haute, on the Wabash
29 "Say, what?"

Puzzle 96

31 Remark from Long John Silver?

32 Place actors don't mind seeing lots of people

34 George Gershwin's "Tee-___-Um-Bum-Bo"

35 Nehi lover of the 4077th

36 When they get smashed, they split on you

38 Kanga's tyke

39 Successfully persuade

44 Third Greek letters

46 Rorschach images

47 Bones once called cubiti

48 Land or sea ending

50 Shake your booty holding an Etch A Sketch

51 Picadors pick on them

52 Wiggle a carrot in front of

54 "Here comes trouble!"

57 Mental ability

58 It's for tat

59 It's fine for NASA

60 401, to Caesar

61 Rapid transit plane, no longer in use

WE DON'T NEED NO STINKIN' THEME!

ACROSS

1 Follows a recipe direction
6 Resort in the Ardennes
9 Ermine, in summer
14 West Indian religious charm
15 Mother ptarmigan
16 Set aside till later
17 To make an excuse in London, say
20 Firm and resolute
21 Having wings
22 Serpentine swimmer
23 Barely achieve, with "out"
24 Coal dust
25 Showing a lack of care for consequences
31 Obeyed Master
33 Its area is about 3.7 million square miles
34 Have something the matter
35 Far more than unpopular
36 Humorously sarcastic
37 Like Glenn Close's attraction for Michael Douglas
39 Rathskeller fare
40 Get entangled in details, with "down"
41 They make bundles
42 They may be tossed around the gym
46 Spellbound
47 South African golfer Ernie
48 "Robin Hood: ___ in Tights"
51 Drama starring Joe Pesci and Sharon Stone
54 Type of pay, after deductions
56 One stirring up trouble for management
58 Get gussied up fussily
59 It's at its best when it's boring
60 Link with
61 Scottish whip
62 Wear and tear
63 Looks that lookers get

DOWN

1 Wedding vow word
2 Reduce in intensity
3 Made a counterattack
4 It may be registered
5 Came clean?
6 Doesn't hog
7 Strike relentlessly, as hail
8 Punk/folk singer DiFranco
9 Stable sections
10 Japanese teahouse mat
11 News item for a scrapbook
12 Shower gel ingredient
13 Man the bar
18 Kind of prey in a Cornel Wilde film title
19 Turkish bath
24 Teapot cover
26 Agatha Christie's "A Pocket Full of ___"
27 Clear of a charge
28 "Psycho" setting
29 Word for Jim Carrey, in a 1997 film
30 These wings don't flap
31 Sam the ___ & the Pharaohs
32 Robert De Niro-Chazz Palminteri film, "A Bronx ___"

36 ". . . ___ you be
my neighbor"
37 Like Adam Sandler's
singing voice
38 Nothing alternative
40 Two-legged support
41 Bronson Pinchot's
"Perfect Strangers" role
43 Where pupils sit, if
you see what I mean
44 Tooth a vampire
prominently displays
45 Snoopy, for one

49 Tread the boards heavily
50 Famous emperor and
famous pianist
51 Cairo Christian
52 That certain something
about someone you
feel, rather than see
53 Hobo concoction,
in stereotypes
54 Fancy shooting marbles
55 Secretary of state
under Reagan
57 The water you drink in Paris

UNIQUE NUMBER

ACROSS

1 Like user-friendly notebook paper
6 Federal organization that may inspect your workplace
10 Not Scary or Baby, the one with Beckham
14 Esteem to the extreme
15 Continuous-play tape
16 First words in the title of Mae West's "angelic" film
17 Captain Hook's "Jolly Roger"
19 Road to Damascus figure, later
20 Greek island that is part of the Cyclades
21 "Switch" or "buck" attachment
22 The "E" in Einstein's formula
24 Greg, to Carol Brady
26 He eulogized Julius
27 Word screamed with joy before "a boy" or "a girl"
28 Orlando's love in "As You Like It"
32 Visually-challenged excavators
35 Greg Louganis' specialty
36 "I saw ___ kissing Kate" (tongue twister)
37 Eurasian range
38 Like wartime messages
39 Eyes a bull's-eye
40 It's gassy and exists to get your attention
41 Breaks new ground
42 When it comes to the atlas, it's not the big picture
43 Questionable patent medicines
45 Snoopy, when wearing his scarf
46 If you have "the ___," you have a strong sexual attraction

47 Hammer and anvil mate
51 Lyricist with Richard Rogers, Hart
54 Dagwood's creator
55 Get some good out of
56 Son of Zeus and Hera
57 Feature of a gas stove, but not an electric one
60 Mild partner?
61 River associated closely with Shakespeare
62 Glowing, smoldering coal
63 Good wine quality
64 Half of an infamous dual personality
65 "Heidi" author Johanna

DOWN

1 Deep blue semiprecious gem
2 Dostoevsky's ding-a-ling
3 It can be found in runes
4 Cenozoic, for one
5 Hates with a passion
6 "Maximus to Gloucester" poet Charles
7 Trendy Manhattan area
8 ___ polloi
9 Mollified
10 Flexible tufted wire for meerschaum users
11 Noted tent tycoon
12 Comfortable and cozy
13 Sacrosanct
18 February 14 figure
23 Org. that sticks to its guns?
25 Half-baked utopia?
26 They're recorded in chess columns
28 Fair offers?
29 Cow-headed goddess of fertility
30 Although you have a first and last, your last is often used

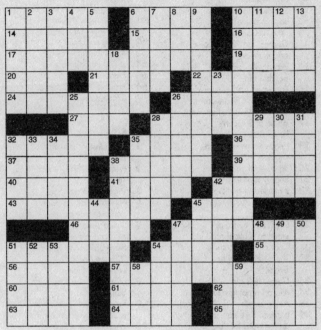

31 Composition of some very dirty clouds

32 He directed Jamie Foxx in both "Miami Vice" and "Collater

33 Little pat on your buns?

34 Vientiane is its capital

35 Destines to a tragic fate

38 Yiddish audacity

42 Eaves droppers?

44 He's right up there with Mick

45 Words with "while you're" or "take a crack"

47 Glittered

48 British sport that resembles American football

49 One who'll help you get with the program?

50 Microorganism-growing dish

51 It's younger than ewe?

52 Cookie sold in a White Fudge version in winter

53 "From Here to Eternity" Oscar winner, Donna

54 Clump of earth

58 It's creepy, but they love it at Wrigley Field

59 Mischievous little rascal

CAPITAL IDEA!

ACROSS

1 Eye swatter?
5 You may test for it by saying "Hello!"
9 "The Fox and the Grapes" or "The Tortoise and the Hare"
14 Word with "each life" or "thin air"
15 Pouchong and gunpowder
16 The Jackson Five wore them everywhere they went
17 Home of Sweden's Royal Ballet
19 Vegas game featuring shooters
20 Small earthen boiler
21 Supply mother's milk
23 It made Jed a millionaire
25 Mother of Ashley and Wynonna
26 Capital of Syria, or where a Biblical road led
31 Coat of arms features
34 The Beatles' "Eight Days ___"
35 Guisewite's girl
37 Blip on a polygraph
38 Ankle-length
39 Nevada lake named for a native word for "big water"
40 Acquire "the old-fashioned way"
41 Noted Verdi aria, "___ tu"
42 Jerry Lewis film, "___ to a Small Planet"
43 Chalet overhangs
44 Small, yellowish-brown variety of pear
46 Capital city at the confluence of the Danube and Sava rivers
48 Dawning
50 Excavated, "Like, . . . understood, man?"
51 Cutting type of kick?
53 Make invalid

58 One way to be wanted, or kicking partner
59 Setting of "Black Hawk Down"
61 Best thing to put on Mediterranean Avenue
62 Voting coalition
63 A stone's throw away
64 Unfathomable chasm
65 Emulate Buffy
66 Brussels-based defense organization

DOWN

1 Thylvethster's thpeech problem
2 Prefix with "body" or "corrosion"
3 Word in an octagon
4 Pawn, or what a poor gambler may be in
5 Italian-American, Mexican-American, etc.
6 Steve Ballmer, at Microsoft
7 "Kiss on My List" partner of Oates
8 Founder of the Ottoman Empire
9 Type of "Girl" in the title of a 2006 Sienna Miller film
10 Inverted-V structure
11 Capital of Slovakia on the Danube River
12 Run in long, smooth, easy strides
13 Superman's logo
18 Stand in the mall?
22 Hidden place, or rhyme for "stash," appropriately
24 Skywalker Ranch owner
26 Agatha Christie and Judi Dench, e.g.
27 Well-apprised, well-informed and with eyes wide open
28 Tenochtitlán, nowadays
29 Series of letters before "O" and "U"

30 Title of respect in colonial India
32 Tuckered out or ready o roll?
33 One of five faculties, six for some
36 Lugged, as a large shopping bag
39 Typical bath flooring
40 Van Gogh had one later in life
42 Blood carriers
43 Pelted with certain ovoid objects
45 Bowie's weapons

47 Marx Brothers trait, or obsolete term for legal insanity
49 What the Pyramids are
51 Oscar Madison, famously
52 What either a hot person or dog is on
54 Ted, the Dolphins first pick in the 2007 NFL draft
55 On open waters
56 Just one of those things?
57 It's worth about a dollar, sometimes more, sometimes less
58 "Eureka!"
60 ___, Daman, and Diu

THEMELESS THINKER

ACROSS
1. Never-ending
10. What padlocks lock
15. Piece of The Rock
16. Prefix with -pedic or -dontic
17. Trojan War prophetess
18. Ersatz chocolate
19. Org. with an oft-quoted journal
20. "Up Where We Belong," for one
21. Radius, but not diameter
22. Theological belief based solely on reason
25. Auction closer?
26. Perry of "House of Payne"
27. Feral cats' haunts
29. One of Caesar's co-stars
31. "The check is in the mail," when it isn't
32. Emerson's "jealous mistress"
33. "The Accidental Tourist" star
34. Denouement
35. The one under God
38. Murphies or spuds
40. No-do connecter
41. "I Want ___ Drug" (Huey Lewis & the News)
43. Extinct flightless bird of New Zealand
44. AK-47 relative
45. One buck, or two
46. Yahoo! but not Google
50. Priests of the East
52. Ball girl who wears two gloves
54. Snail trail
55. Soho baby buggy
56. Phyllis' husband of classic TV
58. Deloitte & Touche partner
59. Tighten brogans
61. Made weak by stunting the growth
64. "___ you so!"
65. Try-before-you-buy computer programs
66. Babe Ruth's number
67. Given life?

DOWN
1. It has a 17-year life cycle
2. Wall or tooth covering
3. Attack with vigor
4. Pension starter?
5. Failed constitutional amendment
6. "The ___ Before Time"
7. Provide, as with a quality
8. Socially-inept "Saved by the Bell" character
9. Marine fish that migrate from salt to fresh water
10. Ad follow-up?
11. "The Sheik of ___" (early tune)
12. It can be very moving to an infant
13. Some shows or song requests
14. Dried out, with "up"
23. Something to put an end to
24. Lots and lots
26. You'll be needled if you get them

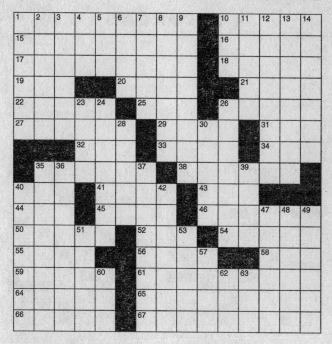

28 Item used in curling
30 What some people
do to your style
35 Home of Mary and Joseph
36 He gave life to Homer
Simpson, and his son
37 Uncalled for
39 Former Chief Justice Warren
40 Anyone who perpetrates
wrongdoing
42 Entwine flowers in a circle
47 Good thing to have with
liver and onions

48 Current name?
49 Like gas you
can't find anymore
51 "Give him an
inch and he'll
take ___"
53 Ron's producing
artner, Glazer
57 Pigeonhole
60 Commune in the
Netherlands
62 Majors in acting?
63 Plant appendage

SOLUTIONS

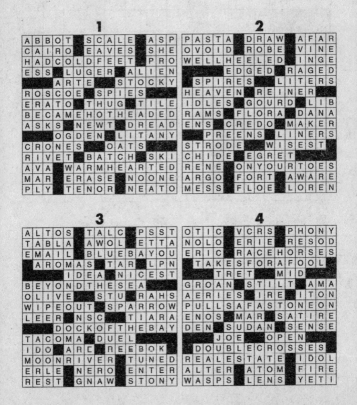

1

A	B	B	O	T		S	C	A	L	E		A	S	P
C	A	I	R	O		E	A	V	E	S		S	H	E
H	A	D	C	O	L	D	F	E	E	T		P	R	O
E	S	S		L	U	G	E	R		A	L	I	E	N
	A	R	T	E		S	T	O	C	K	Y
R	O	S	C	O	E		S	P	I	E	S
E	R	A	T	O		T	H	U	G		T	I	L	E
B	E	C	A	M	E	H	O	T	H	E	A	D	E	D
A	S	K	S		N	E	W	T		D	R	E	A	D
	O	G	D	E	N		L	I	T	A	N	Y
C	R	O	N	E	S		O	A	T	S
R	I	V	E	T		B	A	T	C	H		S	K	I
A	V	A		W	A	R	M	H	E	A	R	T	E	D
M	A	R		E	R	A	S	E		N	O	O	N	E
P	L	Y		T	E	N	O	R		N	E	A	T	O

2

P	A	S	T	A		D	R	A	W		A	F	A	R
O	V	O	I	D		R	O	B	E		V	I	N	E
W	E	L	L	H	E	E	L	E	D		I	N	G	E
	E	D	G	E	D		R	A	G	E	D
S	P	I	R	E	S		L	I	T	E	R	S
H	E	A	V	E	N		R	E	I	N	E	R
I	D	L	E	S		G	O	U	R	D		L	I	B
R	A	M	S		F	L	O	R	A		D	A	N	A
E	N	S		C	R	E	D	O		M	A	K	E	R
	P	R	E	E	N	S		L	I	N	E	R	S
S	T	R	O	D	E		W	I	S	E	S	T
C	H	I	D	E		E	G	R	E	T
R	E	N	E		O	N	Y	O	U	R	T	O	E	S
A	R	G	O		F	O	R	T		A	W	A	R	E
M	E	S	S		F	L	O	E		L	O	R	E	N

3

A	L	T	O	S		T	A	L	C		P	S	S	T
T	A	B	L	A		A	W	O	L		E	T	T	A
E	M	A	I	L		B	L	U	E	B	A	Y	O	U
	A	R	O	M	A	S		T	A	R		L	P	N
	I	D	E	A		N	I	C	E	S	T
B	E	Y	O	N	D	T	H	E	S	E	A
O	L	I	V	E		S	T	U		R	A	H	S
W	I	P	E	O	U	T		S	P	A	R	R	O	W
L	E	E	R		N	S	C		T	I	A	R	A
	D	O	C	K	O	F	T	H	E	B	A	Y
T	A	C	O	M	A		D	U	E	L
I	D	O		A	R	C		R	E	E	B	O	K
M	O	O	N	R	I	V	E	R		T	U	N	E	D
E	R	L	E		N	E	R	O		E	N	T	E	R
R	E	S	T		G	N	A	W		S	T	O	N	Y

4

O	T	I	C		V	C	R	S		P	H	O	N	Y
N	O	L	O		E	R	I	E		R	E	S	O	D
E	R	I	C		R	A	C	E	H	O	R	S	E	S
	T	A	K	E	S	F	O	R	A	F	O	O	L
	T	R	E	T		M	I	D
G	R	O	A	N		S	T	I	L	T		A	M	A
A	E	R	I	E	S		I	R	E		I	T	O	N
P	U	L	L	S	A	F	A	S	T	O	N	E	O	N
E	N	O	S		M	A	R		S	A	T	I	R	E
D	E	N		S	U	D	A	N		S	E	N	S	E
	J	O	E		O	P	E	N
D	O	U	B	L	E	C	R	O	S	S	E	S
R	E	A	L	E	S	T	A	T	E		I	D	O	L
A	L	T	E	R		A	T	O	M		F	I	R	E
W	A	S	P	S		L	E	N	S		Y	E	T	I

5

I	B	E	A	M		B	L	A	B		M	O	L	D
N	A	D	I	A		L	I	R	A		A	M	I	E
D	A	I	R	Y	Q	U	E	E	N		G	A	Z	A
R	E	T		O	U	I		A	D	M	I	R	A	L
I	D	S		R	A	S	P		A	R	C			
		C	A	S	H	R	E	G	I	S	T	E	R	
D	E	N	A	L	I		O	N	E		P	A	R	E
A	X	O	N		D	V	D		E	L	A	N		
S	P	E	D		N	E	O		A	B	L	E	S	T
	H	O	L	Y	M	A	C	K	E	R	E	L		
			C	A	M		E	A	S	Y		G	A	P
S	A	T	A	N	I	C		R	O	O		A	G	O
L	I	O	N		B	R	O	W	N	N	O	S	E	R
O	D	I	E		I	O	W	A		C	H	U	N	K
G	E	L	S		A	P	E	X		E	M	P	T	Y

6

B	U	S		T	H	O	M	E		C	A	R	P	S
E	G	O		W	O	O	E	R		A	L	O	H	A
A	L	L	R	I	G	H	T	A	L	R	E	A	D	Y
D	I	V	A	N			S	O	L	E	D			
L	E	E	J		O	S	W	E	G	O		R	K	O
E	R	R		S	L	I	E	R		M	A	I	L	
			C	L	I	M	B		B	E	A	G	L	E
	T	E	L	E	V	I	S	I	O	N	S	E	T	
D	I	V	I	D	E		I	D	I	O	T			
	D	R	I	P		A	T	O	L	L		R	O	E
T	E	D		P	A	N	E	L	S		P	E	R	U
			E	D	E	N	S			W	I	P	E	R
N	I	N	E	D	O	W	N	O	N	E	T	O	G	O
R	A	C	E	R		E	T	H	E	R		S	O	P
A	N	E	M	O		R	H	O	D	E		E	N	E

7

B	W	A	N	A		A	L	A	S		S	C	A	B
R	I	L	E	S		Z	O	N	E		A	L	T	O
A	T	L	A	S		T	I	E	R		C	A	M	P
W	H	A	T	E	V	E	R	W	O	R	K	S		
L	E	Y		N	I	C	E		L	E	S	S	E	R
			A	T	E		R	O	D		R	A	E	
U	N	S	E	T		S	M	O	G		T	O	M	E
B	Y	H	O	O	K	O	R	B	Y	C	R	O	O	K
O	M	E	N		E	L	S	E		L	I	M	N	S
	A	P	E		A	Y	E		G	E	M			
T	H	R	A	S	H		A	T	O	M		P	S	I
		N	O	H	O	L	D	S	B	A	R	R	E	D
U	S	E	R		L	I	M	A		T	A	U	P	E
R	E	S	T		E	M	I	R		I	N	D	I	A
N	A	S	A		S	O	T	S		S	T	E	A	L

8

F	R	A	U		N	O	V	A		S	E	T	O	N
R	E	S	T		I	B	A	R		L	A	I	N	E
A	N	T	E		L	E	S	S		A	G	R	E	E
M	A	R	R	I	E	D	C	O	U	P	L	E		
E	M	A	I	L		I	O	N	S		E	S	P	N
D	E	Y		O	W	E		S	A	O		O	O	O
			E	V	A	N	S		A	R	M	O	R	
	S	I	L	E	N	T	P	A	R	T	N	E	R	
A	C	T	I	I		A	R	O	M	A				
B	A	A		T	E	A		E	Y	E		A	T	M
E	R	L	E		E	L	L	A		A	S	T	R	O
		I	D	E	N	T	I	C	A	L	T	W	I	N
S	N	A	I	L		A	T	O	P		L	O	C	K
T	E	N	T	S		R	U	D	E		E	R	I	E
P	A	S	S	E		S	P	E	D		O	K	A	Y

9

R	E	C	A	P		C	I	L	I	A		A	X	L
A	M	O	U	R		U	P	E	N	D		R	A	E
S	I	N	G	E	R	D	O	N	N	A		A	N	D
P	R	E		P	O	D		T	S	P		R	A	G
			O	P	A	L	S		T	R	A	D	E	
D	E	C	L	I	N	E	I	N	S	T	A	T	U	S
E	V	A	D	E		L	E	T	O	N				
W	E	B	S		S	E	E	D	Y		S	A	N	D
	A	S	P	E	N		B	O	R	E	R			
N	U	C	L	E	A	R	C	A	L	A	M	I	T	Y
A	N	I	T	A		E	G	A	D	S				
T	I	N		N	F	L		R	I	O		A	R	F
U	T	E		C	O	I	L	E	D	M	E	T	A	L
R	E	M		E	R	N	I	E		E	V	O	K	E
E	R	A		S	T	E	E	D		N	A	M	E	D

10

E	B	B	S		W	A	F	E	R		T	A	M	P
F	O	O	L		A	R	O	M	A		O	V	E	R
T	A	X	I		F	I	R	M	S		M	I	R	O
		S	T	A	T	E	C	A	P	I	T	A	L	S
F	L	U		I	S	L	E		P	R	O	M		
R	A	P	I	D				P	R	O	M			
E	X	P	R	E	S	S	M	A	I	L		S	O	B
R	E	E	K		E	M	I	R	S		E	L	L	E
E	R	R		S	P	E	A	K	E	A	S	I	E	S
			P	E	T	E				M	E	T	O	O
A	I	S	L	E		S	I	R	E		H	S	T	
U	T	T	E	R	N	O	N	S	E	N	S	E		
N	C	A	A		A	R	O	S	E		E	R	A	S
T	H	I	S		S	E	O	U	L		M	E	T	E
S	Y	N	E		H	O	P	E	S		I	D	E	A

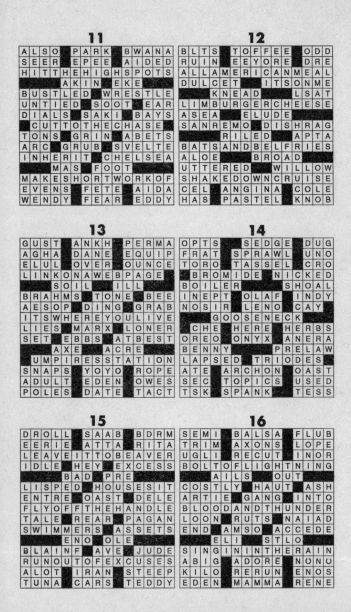

11

A	L	S	O		P	A	R	K		B	W	A	N	A
S	E	E	R		E	P	E	E		A	I	D	E	D
H	I	T	T	H	E	H	I	G	H	S	P	O	T	S
B	U	S	T	L	E	D		W	R	E	S	T	L	E
U	N	T	I	E	D		S	O	O	T		E	A	R
D	I	A	L	S		S	A	K	I		B	A	Y	S
	C	U	T	T	O	T	H	E	C	H	A	S	E	
T	O	N	S		G	R	I	N		A	B	E	T	S
A	R	C		G	R	U	B		S	V	E	L	T	E
I	N	H	E	R	I	T		C	H	E	L	S	E	A
		M	A	S			F	O	O	T				
M	A	K	E	S	H	O	R	T	W	O	R	K	O	F
E	V	E	N	S		F	E	T	E		A	I	D	A
W	E	N	D	Y		F	E	A	R		E	D	D	Y

12

B	L	T	S		T	O	F	F	E	E		O	D	D
R	U	I	N		E	E	Y	O	R	E		D	R	E
A	L	L	A	M	E	R	I	C	A	N	M	E	A	L
D	U	L	C	E	T			I	T	S	O	N	M	E
			K	N	E	A	D				L	S	A	T
L	I	M	B	U	R	G	E	R	C	H	E	E	S	E
A	S	E	A			E	L	U	D	E				
S	A	N	R	E	M	O		D	I	S	H	R	A	G
			R	I	L	E	D			A	P	T	A	
B	A	T	S	A	N	D	B	E	L	F	R	I	E	S
A	L	O	E				B	R	O	A	D			
U	T	T	E	R	E	D		W	I	L	L	O	W	
S	H	A	K	E	D	O	W	N	C	R	U	I	S	E
C	E	L		A	N	G	I	N	A		C	O	L	E
H	A	S		P	A	S	T	E	L		K	N	O	B

13

G	U	S	T		A	N	K	H		P	E	R	M	A
A	G	H	A		D	A	N	E		E	Q	U	I	P
E	L	U	L		O	V	E	R		O	U	N	C	E
L	I	N	K	O	N	A	W	E	B	P	A	G	E	
			S	O	I	L			I	L	L			
B	R	A	H	M	S		T	O	N	E		B	E	E
A	E	S	O	P		D	I	N	G		G	R	A	B
I	T	S	W	H	E	R	E	Y	O	U	L	I	V	E
L	I	E	S		M	A	R	X		L	O	N	E	R
S	E	T		E	B	B	S		A	T	B	E	S	T
			A	X	E			A	C	R	E			
	U	M	P	I	R	E	S	S	T	A	T	I	O	N
S	N	A	P	S		Y	O	Y	O		R	O	P	E
A	D	U	L	T		E	D	E	N		O	W	E	S
P	O	L	E	S		D	A	T	E		T	A	C	T

14

O	P	T	S			S	E	D	G	E		D	U	G
F	R	A	T		S	P	R	A	W	L		U	N	O
T	O	R	O		T	A	S	S	E	L		C	R	O
	B	R	O	M	I	D	E		N	I	C	K	E	D
B	O	I	L	E	R			S	H	O	A	L		
I	N	E	P	T		O	L	A	F		I	N	D	Y
N	O	S	I	R		L	E	N	O		C	A	Y	
			G	O	O	S	E	N	E	C	K			
C	H	E		H	E	R	E		H	E	R	B	S	
O	R	E	O		O	N	Y	X		A	N	E	R	A
B	E	N	N	Y			P	R	E	L	A	W		
L	A	P	S	E	D		T	R	I	O	D	E	S	
A	T	E		A	R	C	H	O	N		O	A	S	T
S	E	C		T	O	P	I	C	S		U	S	E	D
T	S	K		S	P	A	N	K			T	E	S	S

15

D	R	O	L	L		S	A	A	B		B	D	R	M
E	E	R	I	E		A	T	T	A		R	I	T	A
L	E	A	V	E	I	T	T	O	B	E	A	V	E	R
I	D	L	E		H	E	Y		E	X	C	E	S	S
			B	A	D		P	R	E					
L	I	S	P	E	D		H	O	U	S	E	S	I	T
E	N	T	R	E		O	A	S	T		D	E	L	E
F	L	Y	O	F	F	T	H	E	H	A	N	D	L	E
T	A	L	E		R	E	A	R		P	A	G	A	N
S	W	I	M	M	E	R	S		A	S	S	E	T	S
			E	N	O			O	L	E				
B	L	A	I	N	E		A	V	E		J	U	D	E
R	U	N	O	U	T	O	F	E	X	C	U	S	E	S
A	L	O	T		I	R	A	N		S	T	E	E	P
T	U	N	A		C	A	R	S		T	E	D	D	Y

16

S	E	M	I		B	A	L	S	A		F	L	U	B
T	R	I	M		A	X	O	N	S		L	O	P	E
U	G	L	I		R	E	C	U	T		I	N	O	R
B	O	L	T	O	F	L	I	G	H	T	N	I	N	G
			A	I	L	S			O	U	T			
C	O	S	T	L	Y		H	A	U	T		A	S	H
A	R	T	I	E		G	A	N	G		I	N	T	O
B	L	O	O	D	A	N	D	T	H	U	N	D	E	R
L	O	O	N		R	U	T	S		N	A	I	A	D
E	N	D		A	M	S	O		A	C	C	E	D	E
			E	L	I			S	T	L	O			
S	I	N	G	I	N	I	N	T	H	E	R	A	I	N
A	B	I	G		A	D	O	R	E		N	O	N	U
K	I	L	O		R	E	R	U	N		E	N	O	S
E	D	E	N		M	A	M	M	A		R	E	N	E

17

```
B R A D ▪ C O A T I ▪ P E E L
L E N A ▪ A V I A N ▪ H A V E
O D O R ▪ P U R R S ▪ A S I A
C O N T R O L Y O U R S E L F
▪ ▪ ▪ O N E ▪ ▪ L I E ▪ ▪ ▪
O N E D G E ▪ Q U A D ▪ P T A
M O X I E ▪ M A S T ▪ I R O N
A L T E R N A T E E N D I N G
H A R T ▪ E G A D ▪ O O Z E S
A N A ▪ F A I R ▪ A B L E S T
▪ ▪ ▪ S I R ▪ ▪ A L L ▪ ▪ ▪
D E L E T E J U N K E M A I L
I W O N ▪ A O R T A ▪ E U R O
R E D S ▪ S K E I N ▪ S T A B
T R E E ▪ T E A S E ▪ H O N E
```

18

```
D O Z E ▪ D E B T ▪ I M A M S
A K I N ▪ U S E R ▪ B I J O U
M I N D ▪ N C A A ▪ I N A N E
S E C O N D A R Y ▪ D U R S T
▪ ▪ ▪ N O E L ▪ S T E T ▪ ▪
B A N ▪ R E A L ▪ O M E L E T
O M A H A ▪ T A S S ▪ M I L E
R I C O ▪ S O D A S ▪ A R I A
E C R U ▪ P R E F ▪ G N A T S
S I E R R A ▪ N E M O ▪ S E E
▪ ▪ G I N A ▪ T E E M ▪ ▪ ▪
S C O L D ▪ D A Y D R E A M S
P A P A L ▪ A I N U ▪ D R A T
A M U S E ▪ I D E S ▪ A C M E
M E S S Y ▪ R A T A ▪ L O A M
```

19

```
T A P E ▪ L A S S O ▪ ▪ C H E
A B E L ▪ O S K A R ▪ A B E D
M O T E ▪ A L I A S ▪ B E A D
P R I V A T E P R O P E R T Y
A T T A C H E ▪ ▪ ▪ N E T ▪
▪ S E T H ▪ P O P ▪ A S T E R
▪ ▪ E O N ▪ L I P ▪ ▪ A C E
P E R S O N A L P R O N O U N
O V A ▪ ▪ E L I ▪ O N E ▪ ▪
T E N S E ▪ L E T ▪ T O M S ▪
▪ E L S ▪ ▪ ▪ R O A N O K E
I N T I M A T E A P P A R E L
C O R N ▪ F A R C E ▪ T O E S
E R I E ▪ E L L E N ▪ A S T I
D A M ▪ ▪ S E E R S ▪ L E S E
```

20

```
W R A T H ▪ M E S H ▪ A B B A
H A N E Y ▪ O L I O ▪ S E A M
E N G A G E D I N B A T T L E
L E E ▪ I N E Z ▪ O R E A D S
P E R M E D ▪ A S K E R ▪ ▪
▪ ▪ A N E W ▪ P E A N U T S
L O C K E D H O R N S ▪ P H I
I D L E ▪ I D I ▪ ▪ S T A R
M O E ▪ C A M E T O B L O W S
P R O F E S S ▪ E P E E ▪ ▪
▪ ▪ L L O Y D ▪ T H W A R T
E N G U L F ▪ A G I O ▪ B A A
T O O K O N A L L C O M E R S
A N N E ▪ O R E O ▪ V A L E T
L E G S ▪ W I S P ▪ E V E R Y
```

21

```
I N T O ▪ H A R M S ▪ S G T S
D U O S ▪ E S S A Y ▪ A R A T
A M E S ▪ D I V A N ▪ Y O R E
▪ S T O P G A P M E A S U R E
T K O ▪ D E N ▪ ▪ L O N E R
O U T T A ▪ A E R I ▪ D D S
F L O E ▪ W A N N A B E ▪ ▪
F L E E T I N G G L I M P S E
▪ ▪ M A L T E S E ▪ M O O N
A M O ▪ K T E L ▪ F E R M I
P E K O E ▪ C D S ▪ T E D
P A S S I N G T H O U G H T ▪
A N A T ▪ O N I O N ▪ R O I L
L I N E ▪ M U N R O ▪ A L M A
L E A R ▪ E S T E R ▪ D E E D
```

22

```
S O W ▪ S C A L A ▪ B E L L E
N U I ▪ T O M E S ▪ A G A I N
A T L ▪ O V E N S ▪ C O W E D
F I D D L E S T I C K S ▪ ▪
U N S E E N ▪ O S U ▪ R I D
▪ ▪ S N A P ▪ T E M P U R A
H O O P ▪ N A B ▪ A A R O N
O R G A N T R A N S P L A N T
R A D I O ▪ G I T ▪ E L S E
S T E R N E R ▪ P A S T ▪ ▪
E E N ▪ R U M ▪ M U T U A L
▪ ▪ H O R N O F P L E N T Y
A E S O P ▪ S T E E L ▪ F A R
P R O S E ▪ T I L D E ▪ I R E
E A T E N ▪ O F T E N ▪ T I S
```

23

B	A	U	D		F	E	E	D	S		B	A	S	H
T	U	N	E		A	T	T	I	C		A	S	T	A
U	N	D	E	R	L	O	C	K	A	N	D	K	E	Y
	T	O	P	E	S		E	T	A	G	E	R	E	
			V	E	S	T		M	E	D	E	S		
T	A	M	P	A		C	O	L	D	E	R			
I	D	I	O	M		A	W	A	Y		M	A	E	
M	A	N	I	P	U	L	A	T	E	S	T	O	C	K
	E	M	T		M	A	R	E		T	O	R	R	E
			S	H	A	R	D	S		A	N	N	E	S
O	M	A	H	A		S	T	A	T					
R	E	C	I	T	A	L		P	E	O	N	S		
B	A	R	R	E	L	O	F	M	O	N	K	E	Y	S
E	R	I	K		D	R	E	A	R		R	E	N	O
D	A	D	S		A	N	E	N	T		A	D	E	N

24

S	H	E	M	P		B	L	I	N	I		H	O	T
E	A	T	U	P		L	I	V	I	D		A	D	A
G	U	E	S	S	T	I	M	A	T	E		R	I	M
A	S	S	T		U	N	O		W	A	K	E	U	P
			S	A	R	D		D	I	L	E	M	M	A
A	S	S	E	R	T		B	E	T	S	Y			
T	A	K	E	A	L	E	A	P			S	W	A	Y
O	V	A		B	E	D	R	O	C	K		R	I	O
M	E	T	E			I	N	T	H	E	D	A	R	K
			L	O	A	F	S		E	L	A	P	S	E
R	O	Y	A	L	T	Y		I	S	P	Y			
I	S	O	L	D	E		T	N	T		C	A	P	E
L	A	Y		M	A	K	E	A	S	T	A	B	A	T
E	G	O		A	S	I	A	N		A	R	E	N	A
Y	E	S		N	E	A	L	E		B	E	T	E	L

25

W	A	R	M		M	A	I	D	S		E	B	A	Y
E	T	U	I		A	S	S	E	T		N	O	R	A
B	E	R	L	I	N	W	A	L	L		T	R	I	P
			E	N	N	A		I	O	D	I	D	E	S
R	A	B	A	T		N	O	V		O	R	E	L	
A	D	A	G	E	S		P	E	S	T	E	R		
T	O	R	E	R	O		I	R	K	S		S	A	D
E	R	R	S		P	E	A	S	E		A	T	N	O
S	E	I		C	U	L	T		E	N	C	A	G	E
		E	L	A	P	S	E		T	A	T	T	E	R
	B	R	A	D		I	S	M		S	U	E	R	S
M	A	R	T	I	A	N		A	S	T	A			
I	S	E	E		C	O	U	N	T	Y	L	I	N	E
L	I	E	S		E	R	A	S	E		L	O	I	N
L	E	F	T		S	E	W	E	R		Y	U	L	E

26

M	U	L	E		W	A	T	E	R		T	R	A	M
A	T	I	E		I	N	A	N	E		W	A	S	I
R	U	M	R	U	N	N	I	N	G		O	P	A	L
T	R	A	I	T			L	E	A	D	P	I	P	E
I	N	S	E	A	M	S		A	L	O	A	D		
			S	H	I	E	L	D		G	I	F	T	S
J	E	S	T		L	E	A		A	I	R	I	N	G
P	A	P		O	L	D	S	A	L	T		R	U	T
E	V	I	N	C	E		S	U	E		P	E	T	S
G	E	N	E	T		S	O	L	V	E	R			
		A	W	A	R	E		D	E	V	I	A	T	E
W	E	L	L	D	O	N	E			A	N	N	U	M
O	S	T	E		C	O	M	M	O	N	C	O	L	D
U	S	A	F		K	R	E	B	S		E	L	S	E
K	E	P	T		S	A	R	A	H		S	E	A	N

27

S	T	A	R	K		C	P	A		T	A	C	K	S
E	R	N	I	E		H	E	P		S	T	R	A	P
C	A	N	D	Y	B	A	R	S		P	L	A	T	O
S	P	A		P	U	M	M	E	L		E	Z	I	O
			W	A	R	P		S	P	R	A	Y	E	R
	G	O	O	D	E	A	R		N	O	S	H		
O	I	N	K		A	G	A	R		A	T	O	L	L
A	L	I		S	U	N	B	E	A	M		R	I	O
F	L	O	R	A		E	A	S	T		I	S	P	Y
		N	O	S	Y		T	I	R	A	D	E	S	
H	A	R	S	H	E	R		D	I	G	S			
U	R	I	S		T	E	R	E	S	A		M	A	E
M	E	N	S	A		B	A	N	K	V	A	U	L	T
A	N	G	E	L		E	T	C		E	L	L	E	N
N	A	S	A	L		L	E	E		S	A	L	S	A

28

F	A	R	S	I		M	I	L	K		C	A	M	E
A	C	O	R	N		O	R	I	N		I	G	O	R
I	N	S	I	D	E	D	O	P	E		R	E	P	O
L	E	E		O	V	E	N		E	M	C	E	E	S
			N	O	E	S		T	H	O	U			
M	A	N	O	R	S		C	R	O	S	S	B	O	W
A	R	A	B	S		C	O	A	L		C	L	X	I
D	O	D	O		S	A	U	C	E		L	A	I	R
A	M	I	D		T	I	L	E		R	O	N	D	E
M	A	R	Y	L	A	N	D		H	A	W	K	E	D
			S	E	R	E		K	I	L	N			
C	O	M	F	I	T		S	E	L	L		O	R	E
O	L	E	O		L	O	C	A	L	Y	O	K	E	L
L	I	M	O		E	T	A	T		E	A	R	N	S
T	O	O	L		D	O	N	S		S	T	A	T	E

29

E	R	G	S		A	R	U	B	A		S	C	A	M
M	E	A	T		C	A	R	O	M		I	R	M	A
B	A	L	O	N	E	Y	S	U	B		L	O	O	N
A	G	O	R	A		S	A	N	E		I	C	K	Y
R	A	R	I	N	G			T	R	U	C	K		
K	N	E	E		A	C	H	Y		S	O	P	H	S
			S	A	M	O	A		P	A	N	O	U	T
N	A	B		B	U	L	L	D	O	G		T	H	Y
T	R	U	A	N	T		V	I	L	E	R			
H	I	N	G	E		S	E	E	K		E	M	I	T
	K	A	R	A	T				A	L	P	A	C	A
G	O	B	I		N	E	A	T		A	R	D	E	N
O	P	E	N		G	A	R	B	A	G	E	C	A	N
L	I	D	S		U	M	A	S	S		S	A	G	E
F	E	S	T		S	Y	L	P	H		S	P	E	D

30

F	A	D	S		I	R	I	S		A	M	A	Z	E
A	L	E	E		N	E	O	N		N	E	V	E	R
L	O	B	E		T	U	T	U		A	R	E	N	A
S	O	U	N	D	A	S	A	B	E	L	L			
E	F	T		A	C	E	S		V	O	I	C	E	S
			G	U	T			S	I	G	N	O	R	A
C	L	E	A	N		S	L	A	T			O	A	K
H	E	A	L	T	H	Y	A	S	A	H	O	R	S	E
E	E	G			E	N	D	S		A	P	S	E	S
A	C	E	R	B	I	C			D	I	T			
T	H	R	E	E	S		A	B	E	T		O	C	T
			F	I	T	A	S	A	F	I	D	D	L	E
R	E	S	I	N		W	I	R	E		I	D	E	A
A	M	O	N	G		O	D	O	R		A	L	A	S
D	U	N	E	S		L	E	N	S		L	Y	R	E

31

N	A	S	A	L		B	R	I	E	F		M	R	I
A	L	U	L	A		A	U	R	A	L		I	A	N
E	L	B	O	W	G	R	E	A	S	E		L	I	T
			T	E	N	O	R		E	X	C	I	S	E
A	P	R		S	W	I	S	S			R	E	I	N
L	E	A	F		N	O	S	E	A	R	O	U	N	D
D	E	C	O	R			W	A	G	O	N			
O	N	T	R	I	A	L		M	E	L	I	S	S	A
			E	L	I	A	S			L	E	M	O	N
L	I	P	S	E	R	V	I	C	E			S	A	F	E
A	G	U	E		A	R	O	M	A			L	A	W
U	N	R	E	A	L		T	I	D	A	L			
R	O	E		F	O	O	T	T	R	A	F	F	I	C
E	R	E		R	A	T	I	O		P	A	R	D	O
L	E	D		O	F	T	E	N		T	R	Y	S	T

32

D	I	O	N		B	A	I	T		P	A	P	A	S
A	B	R	A		A	C	R	E		L	L	A	M	A
D	E	N	M	O	T	H	E	R		A	P	R	I	L
S	T	E	E	L	I	E		M	A	T	I	L	D	A
			L	E	N	D			R	E	N	O		
P	A	G	E	S			M	A	N	N	E	R	E	D
A	L	A	S		M	A	U	V	E	S		G	A	R
S	I	R	S		E	S	S	E	S			L	A	T	E
S	E	A		E	T	H	E	R	S		A	M	E	S
E	N	G	I	N	E	E	R			O	V	E	N	S
			E	N	D	O			S	A	K	I		
O	B	S	C	U	R	E		T	E	A	S	H	O	P
F	L	A	I	R		S	T	U	D	Y	H	A	L	L
F	A	L	S	E		P	I	N	E		E	L	I	A
S	T	E	E	D		Y	A	K	S		D	E	N	Y

33

T	R	Y	S	T		P	E	E	R		A	R	E	A
O	N	A	I	R		E	M	M	A		E	O	N	S
R	A	W	R	E	C	R	U	I	T		R	U	S	T
			M	O	I	S	T			A	G	U	E	
C	A	R	R	O	L	L		T	E	T	H	E	R	
A	B	O	A	R	D		F	E	E	L	E	R		
L	O	C	K	S		B	L	A	N	K		I	C	E
L	I	K	E		M	O	O	R	S		A	D	E	N
A	L	I		L	I	N	E	N		O	R	E	A	D
		N	I	E	C	E	S		A	V	E	R	S	E
S	A	R	N	I	A			B	L	E	S	S	E	D
T	R	O	D		B	A	U	E	R					
R	O	B	E		R	I	F	L	E	R	A	N	G	E
A	M	I	E		O	R	A	L		A	L	O	E	S
W	A	N	D		E	R	R	S		N	E	W	T	S

34

A	R	U	B	A		C	H	A	S	M		T	O	P
L	Y	S	O	L		B	U	R	M	A		A	B	A
B	E	A	T	T	H	E	H	E	A	T		K	E	N
			C	H	A	R		N	R	C		E	L	I
G	A	S	H	E	S		P	A	T	H	E	T	I	C
R	T	E		A	B	B	A	S			B	A	H	
I	R	A	Q		E	A	R		D	O	T	E	R	S
D	I	L	U	T	E	D		L	E	X	I	C	O	N
S	A	T	E	E	N		A	E	R		N	A	P	A
			H	U	R		C	L	O	V	E		K	E	G
C	H	E	E	R	F	U	L		I	M	B	E	D	S
N	O	D		I	R	R		I	S	E	E			
O	W	E		F	I	L	L	T	H	E	B	I	L	L
T	I	A		I	D	E	A	L		R	O	D	E	O
E	E	L		C	A	R	O	L		S	P	A	I	N

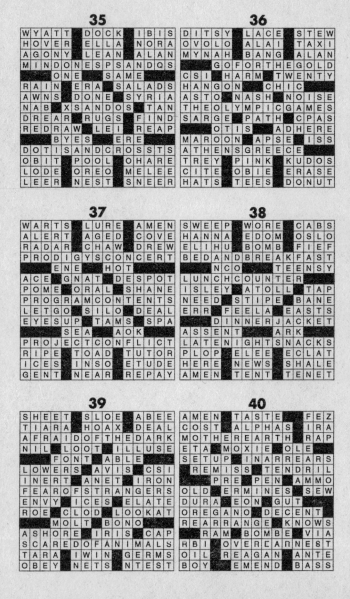

35

W	Y	A	T	T		D	O	C	K		I	B	I	S
H	O	V	E	R		E	L	L	A		N	O	R	A
A	G	O	N	Y		L	E	A	N		A	L	A	N
M	I	N	D	O	N	E	S	P	S	A	N	D	Q	S
			O	N	E			S	A	M	E			
R	A	I	N		E	R	A		S	A	L	A	D	S
A	W	N	S		D	O	N	E		S	Y	R	I	A
N	A	B		X	S	A	N	D	O	S		T	A	N
D	R	E	A	R		R	U	G	S		F	I	N	D
R	E	D	R	A	W		L	E	I		R	E	A	P
			B	Y	E	S			E	R	E			
D	O	T	I	S	A	N	D	C	R	O	S	S	T	S
O	B	I	T		P	O	O	L		O	H	A	R	E
L	O	D	E		O	R	E	O		M	E	L	E	E
L	E	E	R		N	E	S	T		S	N	E	E	R

36

D	I	T	S	Y		L	A	C	E		S	T	E	W
O	V	O	L	O		A	L	A	I		T	A	X	I
M	Y	N	A	H		B	A	N	G		A	L	A	N
		G	O	F	O	R	T	H	E	G	O	L	D	
C	S	I		H	A	R	M		T	W	E	N	T	Y
H	A	N	G	O	N			C	H	I	C			
A	S	T	O		N	A	S	H		N	O	I	S	E
T	H	E	O	L	Y	M	P	I	C	G	A	M	E	S
S	A	R	G	E		P	A	T	H		C	P	A	S
			O	T	I	S		A	D	H	E	R	E	
M	A	R	O	O	N		A	P	S	E		I	S	S
A	T	H	E	N	S	G	R	E	E	C	E			
T	R	E	Y		P	I	N	K		K	U	D	O	S
C	I	T	E		O	B	I	E		E	R	A	S	E
H	A	T	S		T	E	E	S		D	O	N	U	T

37

W	A	R	T	S		L	U	R	E		A	M	E	N
A	L	E	R	T		A	G	E	D		C	O	V	E
R	A	D	A	R		C	H	A	W		D	R	E	W
P	R	O	D	I	G	Y	S	C	O	N	C	E	R	T
			E	N	E			H	O	T				
A	C	E		G	N	A	T		D	E	S	P	O	T
P	O	M	E		O	R	A	L		S	H	A	N	E
P	R	O	G	R	A	M	C	O	N	T	E	N	T	S
L	E	T	G	O		S	I	L	O		D	E	A	L
E	Y	E	S	U	P		T	A	M	S		S	P	A
			S	E	A			A	O	K				
P	R	O	J	E	C	T	C	O	N	F	L	I	C	T
R	I	P	E		T	O	A	D		T	U	T	O	R
I	C	E	S		I	N	S	O		E	T	U	D	E
G	E	N	T		N	E	A	R		R	E	P	A	Y

38

S	W	E	E	P		W	O	R	E		C	A	B	S
H	A	N	N	A		E	D	O	M		O	S	L	O
E	L	I	H	U		B	O	M	B		F	I	E	F
B	E	D	A	N	D	B	R	E	A	K	F	A	S	T
			N	C	O				T	E	E	N	S	Y
L	U	N	C	H	C	O	U	N	T	E	R			
I	S	L	E	Y		A	T	O	L	L		T	A	P
N	E	E	D		S	T	I	P	E		B	A	N	E
E	R	R		F	E	E	L	A		E	A	S	T	S
			D	I	N	N	E	R	J	A	C	K	E	T
A	S	S	E	N	T				A	R	K			
L	A	T	E	N	I	G	H	T	S	N	A	C	K	S
P	L	O	P		E	L	E	E		E	C	L	A	T
H	E	R	E		N	E	W	S		S	H	A	L	E
A	M	E	N		T	E	N	T		T	E	N	E	T

39

S	H	E	E	T		S	L	O	E		A	B	E	E
T	I	A	R	A		H	O	A	X		D	E	A	L
A	F	R	A	I	D	O	F	T	H	E	D	A	R	K
N	I	L		L	O	O	T		I	L	L	U	S	E
			F	O	N	T		A	B	L	E			
L	O	W	E	R	S		A	V	I	S		C	S	I
I	N	E	R	T		A	N	E	T		I	R	O	N
F	E	A	R	O	F	S	T	R	A	N	G	E	R	S
E	N	V	Y		I	C	E	S		E	L	A	T	E
R	O	E		C	L	O	D		L	O	O	K	A	T
			M	O	L	T		B	O	N	O			
A	S	H	O	R	E		I	R	I	S		C	A	P
S	C	A	R	E	D	O	F	A	N	I	M	A	L	S
T	A	R	A		I	W	I	N		G	E	R	M	S
O	B	E	Y		N	E	T	S		N	T	E	S	T

40

A	M	E	N		T	A	S	T	E			F	E	Z
C	O	S	T		A	L	P	H	A	S		I	R	A
M	O	T	H	E	R	E	A	R	T	H		R	A	P
E	T	A		M	O	X	I	E		O	L	E		
S	E	T	U	P			I	N	A	R	R	E	A	R	S
	R	E	M	I	S	S		T	E	N	D	R	I	L
			P	R	E		P	E	N		A	M	M	O
O	L	D		E	R	M	I	N	E	S		S	E	W
D	U	R	A		E	O	N		G	U	T			
O	R	E	G	A	N	O		D	E	C	E	N	T	
R	E	A	R	R	A	N	G	E		K	N	O	W	S
	R	A	M		B	O	M	B	E		V	I	A	
R	B	I		O	V	E	R	C	A	N	N	E	S	T
O	I	L		R	E	A	G	A	N		A	N	T	E
B	O	Y		E	M	E	N	D		B	A	S	S	

41

B	O	A	S	T		M	I	L	O		H	A	T	E
A	L	P	H	A		U	T	A	H		O	V	I	D
B	A	S	E	B	A	L	L	D	I	A	M	O	N	D
U	V	E	A		T	E	L		O	N	E	W	A	Y
			F	E	W		R	A	T	S				
E	B	B		G	A	R	D	E	N	S	P	A	D	E
T	E	A		O	R	E	O	S			U	S	E	R
H	A	N	D	S		D	R	E		I	N	T	W	O
I	N	T	O		E	I	L	A	T		O	E	D	
C	O	U	N	T	R	Y	C	L	U	B		R	Y	E
			A	G	U	E		R	E	V				
L	A	S	T	I	N		M	B	A		E	T	A	S
A	R	T	I	F	I	C	I	A	L	H	E	A	R	T
C	I	A	O		N	O	N	E		O	R	S	E	A
Y	A	R	N		S	E	E	R		E	S	S	A	Y

42

A	C	D	C		B	R	I	N	G		B	R	I	M
T	A	R	A		R	A	T	I	O		R	U	N	E
O	N	E	L		A	N	E	N	T		I	S	L	E
	I	D	I	D	N	T	M	E	A	N	T	H	A	T
			C	A	D	S			L	O	T			
P	R	I	O	R	Y		S	L	O	W		A	R	E
O	U	N	C	E		A	T	O	N		A	R	U	M
P	L	E	A	S	E	F	O	R	G	I	V	E	M	E
P	E	R	T		X	R	A	Y		M	A	N	O	R
A	R	T		S	H	O	T		S	A	L	A	R	Y
			S	U	I			A	L	G	A			
C	A	N	W	E	B	E	F	R	I	E	N	D	S	
O	L	I	O		I	D	I	O	M		C	R	O	P
C	O	C	O		T	E	A	S	E		H	E	R	A
K	E	E	P		A	N	T	E	S		E	W	E	R

43

M	O	P	S		A	M	F	M		B	U	R	R	S
E	R	I	N		P	O	L	O		I	S	A	A	C
A	L	T	O		P	R	O	P	A	G	A	N	D	A
D	O	U	B	L	E	A	G	E	N	T		G	I	N
E	P	I		L	A	Y		S	O	B	E	I	T	
		T	S	A	R		W	H	E	E	L			
C	H	A	I	N		P	A	U	L		A	I	W	A
B	U	R	R	O	W	I	N	G	M	A	M	M	A	L
S	T	Y	E		R	O	E	S		Z	E	B	R	A
			N	O	E	N	D		F	U	S	E		
C	E	S	S	N	A		A	E	R		C	I	S	
O	B	I		S	K	I	N	B	L	E	M	I	S	H
M	O	N	T	E	S	S	O	R	I		O	L	L	A
I	N	G	O	T		I	V	A	N		L	E	A	K
N	Y	E	T	S		S	A	M	E		E	S	M	E

44

R	E	P	R	O		F	E	A	T		A	N	K	A
A	M	O	U	R		A	R	I	A		B	O	O	R
D	I	S	M	I	S	S	A	L	L	D	O	U	B	T
S	T	Y		G	E	T	S		K	I	D	N	E	Y
			F	I	N	E		I	S	E	E			
D	O	S	A	N	D	D	O	N	T	S		T	S	P
U	N	I	T	A	S		Z	O	O		F	R	A	U
M	E	D	A	L		J	A	N		G	U	I	L	T
B	A	L	L		V	O	W		S	O	R	E	S	T
O	L	E		D	A	Y	A	F	T	E	R	D	A	Y
			B	I	N	S		E	A	S	Y			
A	L	C	O	V	E		V	I	S	A		S	P	A
D	U	L	L	A	S	D	I	S	H	W	A	T	E	R
D	R	A	T		S	E	A	T		A	L	A	R	M
S	E	W	S		A	B	L	Y		Y	A	N	K	S

45

C	R	A	W		F	L	I	N	T		S	L	O	P
A	I	D	A		A	U	D	I	O		C	O	P	E
S	L	A	Y		I	C	E	B	R	E	A	K	E	R
E	L	M	S		L	I	S		A	T	I	L	T	
		A	I	M	E	D		M	I	S	T			
L	A	N	D	E	D		T	A	S	T	E	B	U	D
E	L	D	E	R		H	A	I	L		R	I	P	E
A	T	E		H	A	L	L	E		S	P	A		
S	A	V	E		E	Y	E	S		O	T	H	E	R
T	R	E	S	T	L	E	S		S	P	O	O	R	S
			T	O	P	S		S	I	T	U	P		
A	B	E	A	M		R	O	C		T	S	A	R	
B	U	T	T	E	R	M	I	L	K		E	C	R	U
L	O	N	E		C	A	N	A	L		R	A	I	N
E	Y	A	S		A	N	D	R	E		S	P	A	T

46

S	O	P	S		D	A	R	E	S		S	H	E	D
E	P	E	E		I	D	O	N	T		T	O	T	O
C	U	S	T	O	M	M	A	D	E		O	N	U	S
	S	T	A	R	W	A	R	S	W	O	O	K	I	E
			D	I	N			O	W	L				
T	I	C	K	E	T		R	O	V	E		J	A	B
O	S	H	E	A		S	E	R	E		P	O	L	L
P	L	A	Y	L	I	K	E	A	R	O	O	K	I	E
P	E	N	S		C	E	L	L		R	E	E	V	E
S	S	T		P	E	W	S		H	A	T	R	E	D
			A	R	C			S	O	T				
O	N	E	T	O	U	G	H	C	O	O	K	I	E	
G	O	G	O		B	E	D	O	F	R	O	S	E	S
R	E	I	N		E	N	T	R	E		R	A	G	E
E	L	S	E		S	A	V	E	D		N	O	S	E

47

```
B O L L   B E I N G   S I N S
A R E A   E S S E N   A L O E
S T I C K Y S I T U A T I O N
E S S   H O E S     P I A N O
    M A N X   B L A N D E R
A T T E N D   B O O T Y
D O R A   C O N C H   S O N
A F I N E H O W D O Y O U D O
M U G   F A R E S   A I D S
    P L I E D   C U R T S Y
A E R I A L S   H E R S
S L A N T   S A R A   O A K
H O R N S O F A D I L E M M A
E P E E   W A G E S   R E E L
N E R D   E R A S E   A N N E
```

48

```
R U T S   A M E B A   P S S T
E R I N   L A S E D   U P T O
E S A U   T O P A Z   P A R T
B U R G L A R Y D E V I C E
O L A   U R I     C L E A N
K A S E M   P E A R   A M A
    R E D D E E R   O G E E
G U I T A R P L U C K E R
J A N E   R A P S T A R
I D S   I N M Y   M A C A W
F A T A L   B E E   A B A
B A S K E T B A L L P L O Y
M O B S   L E A S E   E L A L
R U L E   M A N I C   T E R A
S T E T   S M E L T   E D D Y
```

49

```
M A T H   E C L A T   P L E D
A C R E   N O O S E   E A S Y
T H U M B S D O W N   R I S E
S E E   R U S S O   E I D E R
    D U E     O C A S
S P A I N   H A N D S H A K E
C A T S T A I L   R E A G A N
R I O T   S E T T O   B A R T
A S L E E P   H O M E L I E R
P A L M P I L O T   L E N N Y
    P I C A   A D S
A Z T E C   M O I R E   P R E
N E A R   F I N G E R F O O D
D A M E   A N T O N   U G L I
S L E D   A G O R A   M O L T
```

50

```
A H A S   B A R K   R E A C H
P E N H   O V A L   E M O R Y
T H A I   L O G E   W I R E D
  C L E A N U P H I T T E R
B L O O M     T E N   A D O
W A S H I N G T O N D C
A G T   R E A R   S P R I T
N O I R   A M U S E   R E N E
A S A N A   M E T S   P A X
  S W E E P A C C O U N T
E M U   A R C   U R G E S
D U S T I N H O F F M A N
I N U I T   O G R E   N A P E
T R A D E   E L A N   G N A T
S O L E D   S E N D   E T N A
```

51

```
R A N D D   I R I S   U P S
O C O M E   G E N R E   P R E
S T E V E A U S T I N   H O E
S O L   P L A T O   C R O W D
I R S   E E N   W O O L
  O S C A R M A D I S O N
A L E R T   U R G E   T W O
M O L E   P O S S E   B E E T
I C E   B I O S   B O R N E
R I V E R P H O E N I X
  A V I S   L A C   L E E
A C T E D   D A I S Y   O R R
M O I   A L A N J A C K S O N
I D O   L I N D A   L E E D S
D A N   D A S H   E G R E T
```

52

```
E F T S   F D I C   S A S H
R I O T   R I N D S   P L E A
E X P E R I E N C E   A L E S
  P O D S   A D D R E S S
U R S U L A   T S A R   G A L
S I M P L Y T H E N A M E W E
E M U   S E E   S K I
R E G A L   A T E   E L F I N
  R O C   I L E   A D O
G I V E O U R M I S T A K E S
A B A   T R E E   C H E E S Y
M E L I S S A   R O A R
B R E D   O S C A R W I L D E
L I T E   R O U S T   A Y E S
E A S E   N E S S   L E N S
```

53

```
P E W S   B R A S S   C O A T
O R A L   L E V E L   H A T S
E I R E   E V E R Y   U R S A
M E D D L E S     F R E E R
      T E D   R O T U N D A S
H O S E A   R A T O N
A T L A S   A T O M   S E R A
F R O M T O P T O B O T T O M
T A B S   P I L L   N E A T O
      R E N E E   E A S E S
F A S T E N E R   H A M
R U P E E     L U M B E R S
I R A N   O L D E R   A L O U
L A N D   Y E A S T   T I M E
L E S S   L I N E S   H E A T
```

54

```
A S A P   S P E N D   S O N S
D E M I   C U R I E   K N I T
D A M N   U T I C A   E T N A
  T O W T R U C K D R I V E R
      H A R P     B A N
N A M E L Y   S E E M   P A R
A D I E U   E L L A   M A G I
P U L L S O M E S T R I N G S
E L K S   F I D E   U N T I E
S T Y   E F T S   A M U S E S
      A S S   O R B S
D R A G S T R I P R A C E S
R A V E   A O R T A   U N T O
I N O N   G A M I N   L I A R
P I N T   E N A C T   E D G E
```

55

```
L I M P   S K I E D   P I N S
A S E A   P A D R E   R O I L
M A R C   A T E I N   O N L Y
B A C K B R E A K I N G
S C H U L E     M O R A L E
  A P A   M O A   R E D I D
F A N   H A I R R A I S I N G
L E T S   S N A K Y   S N E E
A R M T W I S T I N G   F D R
T I A R A   K E N   E L I
T E N A C E     C R A N I A
  F O O T S T O M P I N G
J E D I   S O A R S   E T O N
A M E N   I N G O T   L U N E
R U N G   N E E D S   S M E W
```

56

```
A L T A R   V I N O   S T A T
T E R N E   E V E N   H I V E
R A I N F O R E S T   A G E E
A R G U E R S   T A M P E R S
      A R E A S   R U E R
A M B L E S   T O G S   W O E
B O U L E   E L S E S   O U S
R O S Y   F A U L T   P O T S
A S H   D I S C O   H O D G E
M E L   O N E I   L E S S O N
      E H U D   A E O N S
I N A T R A P   A L R I G H T
C A G E   J U N G L E B O O K
B T U S   O R A L   I L O S T
M E E T   B E B E   D Y N E S
```

57

```
B O O S   S H I E L D   H A M
A B U T   T A R T A R   E V A
H O T A N D H E A V Y   L O N
T E S T A   A S T I   D E N Y
      U S A     S T A N
  C R E A M O F T H E C R O P
O R O   P U R E   S H E L L
S A L S A   T O N   S A D I E
S M E A R   O D O R   D V D
A P P L E O F O N E S E Y E
    L E A R     S H A
A L A S   N E I N   A R T I E
D A Y   H A R D A N D F A S T
A V E   A T M O S T   U L N A
M A R   W E A L T H   L E T S
```

58

```
R E B O P   A S T I R   T W O
O L I V E   C H I V A L R I C
S A N A N D R E A S F A U L T
E N D   P O E M     D E L E
      T A M S   A M H E R S T
S I M I L E   T W A I N
U R A L   T R A C K   I R E
V I C T O R I A S S E C R E T
S S E   D I T C H   L O A N
P I T H Y   A G E N D A
M A T I N E E   S E R F
O V E N   A L O E   C U E
M A R T H A S V I N E Y A R D
M I N O R S U I T   N O R S E
A L S   S H E D S   S U D A N
```

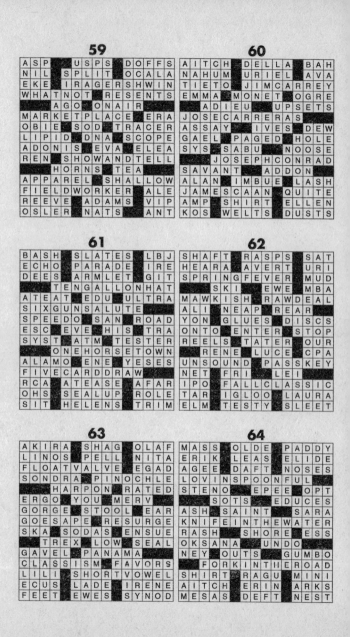

59

```
A S P   U S P S   D O F F S
N I L   S P L I T   O C A L A
E K E   I R A G E R S H W I N
W H A T N O T   R E S E N T S
    A G O   O N A I R
M A R K E T P L A C E   E R A
O B I E   S O D   T R A C E R
L I P I D   D N A   S C O P E
A D O N I S   E V A   E L E A
R E N   S H O W A N D T E L L
    H O R N S   T E A
A P P A R E L   S H A L L O W
F I E L D W O R K E R   A L E
R E E V E   A D A M S   V I P
O S L E R   N A T S   A N T
```

60

```
A I T C H   D E L L A   B A H
N A H U M   U R I E L   A V A
T I E T O   J I M C A R R E Y
E M M A   M O N E T   O G R E
    A D I E U   U P S E T S
J O S E C A R R E R A S
A S S A Y   I V E S   D E W
G A E L   P A G E D   H O L E
S Y S   S A B U   N O O S E
    J O S E P H C O N R A D
S A V A N T   A D D O N
A L A N   I M B U E   L A S H
J A M E S C A A N   Q U I T E
A M P   S H I R T   E L L E N
K O S   W E L T S   D U S T S
```

61

```
B A S H   S L A T E S   L B J
E C H O   P A R A D E   I R E
D E E S   A R M L E T   G I T
    T E N G A L L O N H A T
A T E A T   E D U   U L T R A
S I X G U N S A L U T E
S P E E D O   S A N   R O A D
E S C   E V E   H I S   T R A
S Y S T   A T M   T E S T E R
    O N E H O R S E T O W N
A L A M O   E N E   Y E S E S
F I V E C A R D D R A W
R C A   A T E A S E   A F A R
O H S   S E A L U P   R O L E
S I T   H E L E N S   T R I M
```

62

```
S H A F T   R A S P S   S A T
H E A R A   A V E R T   U R I
S P R I N G F E V E R   M U D
    S K I   E W E   M B A
M A W K I S H   R A W D E A L
A L I   N E A P   R E A R
Y O N   G L U E S   D I S C S
O N T O   E N T E R   S T O P
R E E L S   T A T E R   O U R
    R E N E   L U C E   C P A
U N S O U N D   P A S S K E Y
N E T   F R I   L E I
I P O   F A L L C L A S S I C
T A R   I G L O O   L A U R A
E L M   T E S T Y   S L E E T
```

63

```
A K I R A   S H A G   O L A F
L I N O S   P E L L   N I T A
F L O A T V A L V E   E G A D
S O N D R A   P I N O C H L E
    H A R P O N   R A T E D
E R G O   Y O U   M E R V
G O R G E   S T O O L   E A R
G O E S A P E   R E S U R G E
S K A   S O D A S   E N S U E
    T R E X   L O W   S E A L
G A V E L   P A N A M A
C L A S S I S M   F A V O R S
L I L I   S H O R T V O W E L
E C U S   L A D E   I R E N E
F E E T   E W E S   S Y N O D
```

64

```
M A S S   O L D E   P A D D Y
E R I K   L E A S   E L I D E
A G E E   D A F T   N O S E S
L O V I N S P O O N F U L
S T E N O   E P E E   O P T
    S O T S   E D U C E S
A S H   S A I N T   S A R A
K N I F E I N T H E W A T E R
R A S H   S H O R E   E S S
O K S A N A   U N D O
N E Y   O U T S   G U M B O
F O R K I N T H E R O A D
S H I R T   R A G U   M I N I
A I T C H   E R I N   A R K S
M E S A S   D E F T   N E S T
```

65

```
D E E M ■ C H A S E ■ B L O B
U L V A ■ O I L E R ■ A O N E
G L E N ■ C L E A R ■ C M O N
■ A N I M A L C R A C K E R S
■ ■ ■ A R C ■ ■ S T U B ■ ■ ■
D S T ■ T O L D ■ A P O D A L
A T O P ■ L O O K ■ P A U L A
V E G E T A B L E G A R D E N
I N A N E ■ S T L O ■ D E C K
D O S I N G ■ S P A N ■ S K Y
■ ■ ■ T O R I ■ L E A ■ ■ ■
M I N E R A L D E P O S I T ■
E D E N ■ P I A N O ■ O D O R
T E X T ■ E U R O S ■ N O O N
S E T S ■ S M E L T ■ E L K S
```

66

```
A L A N ■ B A J A ■ B A D G E
T A R O ■ O L L A ■ A D I E U
E X C E L S I O R ■ S O L A R
■ ■ ■ X E N A ■ A S S U R E
S E P I A ■ S E A T O ■ T E K
M T E T N A ■ Y U L ■ V E D A
U R E ■ C I N E R A M A ■ ■ ■
E P L U R I B U S U N U M
■ ■ ■ S T R E A M E D ■ R I O
D A R T ■ A L L ■ S W A N K Y
I V E ■ A I S L E ■ A N S E L
R O L A N D ■ B A S K ■ ■ ■
I C I N G ■ O R O Y P L A T A
G E S T E ■ A O N E ■ E X E C
O T H E R ■ K E Y S ■ T E X T
```

67

```
A C C R A ■ O M A R ■ R C M P
D R Y A D ■ N I L E ■ E L I E
D U S T J A C K E T ■ D O N T
E S T ■ U L E E ■ I S S U E S
R E S O R T ■ T R I E D ■ ■
■ W E A R T H E P A N T S
A P S E ■ R A R A ■ ■ I R E
S E C S ■ S P O T S ■ A N E W
P R O ■ ■ I T C H ■ N E S S
S T U F F E D S H I R T ■
■ ■ T I E R S ■ M I S L E D
A R C A N A ■ E B O N ■ O L E
C Y A N ■ S T R O N G S U I T
M A R C ■ E A T S ■ U N I T E
E S S E ■ D I E S ■ P O S E R
```

68

```
A M O K ■ E A T E R ■ C H A T
K I L N ■ A M B L E ■ O A T H
A S E A ■ S O A K S ■ L I E U
■ T O P S E C R E T F I L E S
■ ■ ■ S T L O ■ ■ O O N ■ ■
C E D A R S ■ G A R R ■ P A W
A M I C E ■ B A S E ■ W A S H
P E A K P E R F O R M A N C E
E R N S ■ M I F F ■ A R D O R
R Y E ■ A B E E ■ B O R A T E
■ ■ O L A ■ ■ H E R A ■ ■ ■
S U M M I T M E E T I N G S ■
A L O E ■ T O A S T ■ T U N A
G A N G ■ L A S S O ■ E R I C
A N K A ■ E N T E R ■ D U P E
```

69

```
A B E T ■ P E S T ■ A B C S
S A G A ■ A N T E ■ S P R A T
S M O K I N J O E ■ L O O S E
■ ■ E N D O W ■ R E L A T E
S O S ■ D A Y ■ F I E L D E R
E C H O E S ■ B E S T O W ■
R H O N E ■ B R I E ■ A C T
G R E E D ■ L O G ■ S T Y L E
E E L ■ M U O N ■ C A J U N
■ E S T E E M ■ B A R O N S
A S S A I L S ■ H E M ■ E K E
M I S L E D ■ H E A P S ■ ■
A N J O U ■ J O L T I N J O E
S C O O P ■ A B L E ■ O A T S
S E E N ■ N O O N ■ B I O S
```

70

```
A B O R T ■ A R O M A ■ T E D
D O W E R ■ P I S A N ■ U N A
D A N C E W I T H M E ■ R I N
■ ■ ■ E B O A T ■ A M A N D A
E P S I L O N ■ E C O L I ■
S H A V E D ■ C R A N S T O N
C A V E ■ H O U S E ■ L I E
U S E R ■ C A R P S ■ S O L I
D E T ■ I L L A T ■ T O M S
O D O N N E L L ■ C E A S E S
■ N O V A E ■ T E R R E N E
G U I T A R ■ A U D I T ■ ■
E R G ■ D O N T B E C R U E L
A S H ■ E U B I E ■ A E T N A
R A T ■ S T A T S ■ S K E E T
```

71

```
P I T A   S T R A W   M R E D
I R O N   L E A S E   A O N E
E A S T   E N G E L   L O O K
R E S O L U T E   C A C K L E
      N E T S   S O L O
R A D I S H   T I M A L L E N
O L I O   L A T E   M A R I
G A R B   G I L E S   M I R E
E T T A   O N U S   C R O C
R E Y N O L D S   F I D D L E
      D A D A   H A L O
S U P E R B   B A C K W A R D
U S S R   L A U R A   E R I E
M E S A   U R G E D   L I M N
O R T S   M A S S E   L A S T
```

72

```
M E W L S   L A Z E   L A L A
A D I E U   O L E O   A M E X
L I N E N   S U P E R B O W L
I T S   S K I M P   E E R I E
      S H I N   E N D L E S S
L O O K I N G G L A S S
O G L I N G   R I G     U S E
C R E P E   F A N   T E S T Y
K E G   A R I   P A L M E R
      L I C E N S E P L A T E
A T L A S E S   U K E S
T R I T E   H O P E D   M D S
B U T T E R C U P   E M A I L
A C H E   B U R L   C A R V E
T E E S   I T S Y   K N E A D
```

73

```
E T U I   N E H R U   A J A R
B O N N   A M A I N   N E M O
B U T T E R C U P S   A L I T
S T O O P   E L A N   G L E E
      N O S E   A W R Y
R E J E C T   A L P H A B E T
E R A   H O R N E   O M E G A
C A M P   P A I N T   S A R K
A S S E S   I S A A C   N E E
P E E P H O L E   C R E S T S
      S T A R   N O U N
M E S A   C L I O   M O I S T
E M I L   H O N E Y B U N C H
A M O K   I L O N A   G L U E
T A N S   D A N D Y   H A T E
```

74

```
E T H E L   A C T S   O M E N
N A O M I   F R E T   P A P A
A B O I L   R O T E   U T A H
C O T T A G E C H E E S E
T O E   B U S   E L S   R O E
    R A N C H D R E S S I N G
      L E K   W E D   T A C O
A L T E R   R E D   W A L E S
B A R R   F E E   L E I
C H A T E A U B R I A N D
S R I   R N S   A O K   E R A
    L O G C A B I N S Y R U P
L A M B   I B I S   P A I N S
O D I E   E L K E   O L D I E
W A X Y   S E E D   T E E N S
```

75

```
S H A M E   B L E W   T E A
P I X E L   R A N I   A R M Y
I G L O O   A K I N   L U P E
T H E W I C K E D W I T C H
E S S   S H E   I M O K A Y
      L E I   L A N A   S S E
S S I   L I E F   G O T I T
T H E W I Z A R D O F O Z
C A I N E   O D O R   A P E
U R N   D A D S   A N N
D E B I T S   T W O   R A P
D O R O T H Y A N D T O T O
N O N O   R A S H   S A G A S
O W E N   O L E O   A X E L S
R N S   S O R E   T I T L E
```

76

```
R A R E   G O B A D   A C R E
A S E A   O L I V E   C O A X
I T S G O O D T O B E H O M E
S H E E R S   S I T U   L O T
E M E R G E D   R O G A I N E
D A D   B O B   R E D D E R
      S E A D O G   N A G S
      I T S Y O U R D I M E
S N A P   S T A R E S
A P P I A N   S T E   R Y A
N E E D N O T   E N T R E E S
V C R   O B O E   C H I N O S
I T S A L L I N T H E G A M E
L R O N   E L Y S E   O M A N
S E N D   R E A P S   R E N T
```

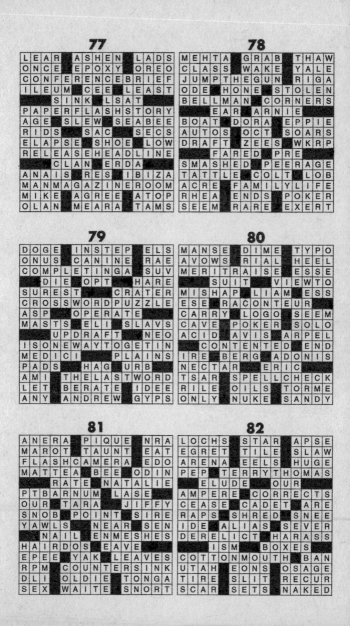

77

```
L E A R   A S H E N   L A D S
O N C E   E P O X Y   O R E O
C O N F E R E N C E B R I E F
I L E U M   C E E   L E A S T
        S I N K   L S A T
P A P E R F L A S H S T O R Y
A G E   S L E W   S E A B E E
R I D S   S A C   S E C S
E L A P S E   S H O E   L O W
R E L E A S E H E A D L I N E
      C L A N   E R D A
A N A I S   R E S   I B I Z A
M A N M A G A Z I N E R O O M
M I K E   A G R E E   A T O P
O L A N   M E A R A   T A M S
```

78

```
M E H T A   G R A B   T H A W
C L A S S   W A K E   Y A L E
J U M P T H E G U N   R I G A
O D E   H O N E   S T O L E N
B E L L M A N   C O R N E R S
      E A R   A R N I E
B O A T   D O R A   E P P I E
A U T O S   O C T   S O A R S
D R A F T   Z E E S   W K R P
      F A R E D   P R E
S M A S H E D   P E E R A G E
T A T T L E   C O L T   L O B
A C R E   F A M I L Y L I F E
R H E A   E N D S   P O K E R
S E E M   R A R E   E X E R T
```

79

```
D O G E   I N S T E P   E L S
O N U S   C A N I N E   R A E
C O M P L E T I N G A   S U V
    D I E   O P T   H A R E
S U R E S T   C R A T E R
C R O S S W O R D P U Z Z L E
A S P   O P E R A T E
M A S T S   E L I   S L A V S
    U P D R A F T   N E O
I S O N E W A Y T O G E T I N
M E D I C I   P L A I N S
P A D S   H A G   U R B
A M I   T H E L A S T W O R D
L E T   B E R A T E   I D E E
A N Y   A N D R E W   G Y P S
```

80

```
M A N S E   D I M E   T Y P O
A V O W S   R I A L   H E E L
M E R I T R A I S E   E S S E
    S U I T   V I E W T O
M I S H A P   L I A M   E S S
E S E   R A C O N T E U R
C A R R Y   L O G O   S E E M
C A V E   P O K E R   S O L O
A C I D   A V I S   A R P E L
    C O N T E N T E D   E N D
I R E   B E R G   A D O N I S
N E C T A R   E R I C
T S A R   S P E L L C H E C K
R I L E   O I L S   T O R M E
O N L Y   N U K E   S A N D Y
```

81

```
A N E R A   P I Q U E   N R A
M A R O T   T A U N T   E A T
F L A S H C A M E R A   E D O
M A T T E A   B E E   O D I N
      R A T E   N A T A L I E
P T B A R N U M   L A S E
O U R   T A R A   J I F F Y
S N O B   P O I N T   S I R E
Y A W L S   N E A R   S E N
    N A I L   E N M E S H E S
H A I R D O S   E A V E
E P E E   Y A K   L E A V E S
R P M   C O U N T E R S I N K
D L I   O L D I E   T O N G A
S E X   W A I T E   S N O R T
```

82

```
L O C H S   S T A R   A P S E
E G R E T   T I L E   S L A W
A R E N A   E E L S   H U G E
P E P   T E R R Y T H O M A S
    E L U D E   O U R
A M P E R E   C O R R E C T S
C E A S E   C A D E T   A R E
R A P S   S H R E D   S N E E
I D E   A L I A S   S E V E R
D E R E L I C T   H A R A S S
      I S M   B O X E S
C O T T O N M O U T H   B A N
U T A H   E O N S   O S A G E
T I R E   S L I T   R E C U R
S C A R   S E T S   N A K E D
```

83 84 85 86 87 88

89

I	B	I	D		M	I	S	S	M		A	P	S	E
B	I	L	E		A	L	T	A	R		C	I	E	N
I	O	L	E		P	L	A	N	B		A	L	A	D
S	P	I	R	A	L	S	T	A	I	R	C	A	S	E
E	I	N		K	E	A		G	E	I	S	H	A	
S	C	I	F	I		Y	A	P		C	A	T	E	R
			I	C	E		F	O	E		E	L	S	
	C	O	R	K	S	C	R	E	W	C	U	R	L	
	C	O	N		T	H	O		E	A	P			
A	M	E	S	S		A	S	A		P	S	A	L	M
	R	E	L	A	I	D		T	H	E		R	I	O
W	H	I	R	L	I	N	G	D	E	R	V	I	S	H
A	O	N	E		S	E	O	U	L		D	A	T	A
S	M	E	E		C	H	A	S	M		A	N	E	W
H	E	R	S		S	I	L	K	S		Y	A	N	K

90

U	S	S	R		A	T	O	Z		A	S	K	S
R	H	E	A		P	R	O	V	E		S	H	O	P
N	E	A	L		A	C	R	E	S		C	A	R	E
	F	L	A	S	H	I	N	T	H	E	P	A	N	
T	R	A	I	N	E	E			O	N	E	N	D	
H	E	R	E	T	O	D	A	Y	A	N	D		
E	M	I	R	S			D	A	N	E		P	B	S
T	A	N	S		T	O	M	M	Y		C	A	I	N
A	N	G		L	O	N	I			T	O	R	S	O
	G	O	N	E	T	O	M	O	R	R	O	W		
A	T	L	A	S			N	E	L	S	O	N	S	
S	H	O	R	T	A	N	D	S	W	E	E	T		
P	E	O	N		P	E	R	I	L		L	I	M	E
E	R	N	E		S	E	E	D	S		E	N	O	L
N	E	S	T		E	D	G	E		T	G	I	F	

91

S	C	A	M	P		S	T	A	G		P	A	L	E
A	L	I	B	I		T	E	T	E		I	V	A	N
C	A	R	A	T		O	N	T	O		F	A	D	E
S	P	Y		F	E	A	T	U	R	E	F	I	L	M
			S	A	L	T	S		G	A	L	L	E	Y
A	N	G	E	L	A			R	I	S	E			
F	I	N	A	L	N	O	T	I	C	E		S	M	U
A	L	A	N		A	I	L		S	E	A	S		
R	E	T		F	O	R	M	L	E	T	T	E	R	S
			T	A	N	S		M	E	A	N	E	R	
A	S	S	A	I	L		A	S	I	A	N			
F	U	M	B	L	E	D	B	A	L	L		M	I	G
O	R	E	O		A	R	A	B		E	L	E	G	Y
R	E	A	R		V	A	S	E		A	E	S	O	P
E	R	R	S		E	W	E	R		F	E	A	R	S

92

S	P	I	C		D	A	F	T		C	O	W	L	S
L	A	S	H		A	G	U	E		Y	A	H	O	O
E	R	N	E		P	A	S	S		C	R	I	B	S
W	A	T	E	R	P	I	S	T	O	L		T	B	A
			T	E	E	N	Y		K	E	S	E	Y	
A	U	P	A	I	R			S	A	R	A	H		
S	P	A	H	N		S	K	I	P		D	O	C	K
I	O	C		K	I	N	G	P	I	N		U	R	N
A	N	K	A		N	I	B	S		E	N	S	U	E
		S	T	R	U	T			B	R	E	E	Z	E
	D	A	M	E	S		H	E	A	D	S			
W	E	D		D	E	S	E	R	T	S	T	O	R	M
W	I	D	T	H		H	I	N	T		E	R	I	E
I	G	L	O	O		O	D	I	E		G	A	L	A
I	N	E	P	T		P	I	E	R		G	L	E	N

93

B	L	I	N	D		H	A	S	P		S	A	S	H
L	A	C	E	Y		O	S	L	O		O	T	T	O
A	V	I	A	N		G	A	I	L		N	O	O	N
D	E	N	T	A	L	A	P	P	L	I	A	N	C	E
E	R	G		M	A	N			T	R	E	K	S	
			M	I	X		C	A	D	S		M	I	T
S	W	A	T		A	U	T	O		D	E	N	Y	
	W	A	T	E	R	C	R	O	S	S	I	N	G	
D	A	L	E		A	H	E	M		T	O	T	S	
E	L	L		E	Y	E	D		F	A	R			
S	L	O	P	E		P	I	N		B	E	G		
P	O	P	U	L	A	R	C	A	R	D	G	A	M	E
I	W	I	N		L	O	O	N		I	O	W	A	N
S	E	N	T		D	A	R	T		N	A	D	I	R
E	R	G	S		A	D	D	S		S	T	Y	L	E

94

E	T	A	L		H	U	T	S		C	O	M	E	T
R	A	L	E		O	P	A	H		A	D	O	R	E
I	X	I	A		M	O	L	E		T	I	B	I	A
K	I	T	C	H	E	N	C	L	E	A	N	S	E	R
			H	O	T			F	T	C				
H	B	O		B	O	H	R		C	O	R	S	E	T
O	R	M	E		W	O	O	L		M	A	I	N	E
H	E	A	V	E	N	L	Y	O	R	B	I	T	E	R
O	S	H	E	A		M	A	K	O		D	A	M	S
S	T	A	R	R	Y		L	I	S	A		R	Y	E
			T	E	C			E	L	M				
B	I	L	L	H	A	L	E	Y	B	A	C	K	U	P
A	L	O	U	D		O	L	E	O		J	O	N	I
T	I	A	R	A		S	L	A	W		O	B	I	T
H	A	N	K	Y		E	A	R	L		B	E	T	S

95

```
E F G H I   H A S H   I C O N
T H E O C   O L E O   N A V E
H O R S E D R A W N   A M E S
E L M   D A D S   O F F E R S
R E S T O R E   D R O O L
    O W N   D R A U G H T S
H E M E N   P E A R L   U R I
E M U S   S O F T Y   S M O G
A I L   A P S E S   D E P T H
T R E M B L E R   B E E
  T I L E S   P A C K E T S
W A R D E N   S O S A   M O I
E G A D   D O N K E Y K O N G
R A I L   O B O E   E A T E N
E R N E   R I B S   D Y E R S
```

96

```
P A R A P E T   P R U N I N G
E L E V A T E   A E R O S O L
R E V E N U E   R E N T S T O
    R E D   N O D S   E R S
L I T T L E L U L U   T I E S
U T A     A M E C H E
R A M A   B I B   A U R O R A
C L E A R O N E S T H R O A T
H Y D R O X   R E E   E D D O
    G O O G O L     L A M
B U S H   F A N L E T T E R S
L L C   O F M E   R O E
O N A W H I M   T A R M A C S
T A P I O C A   I S O P O D S
S E E T H E S   T E S T K I T
```

97

```
W A R M S   S P A   S T O A T
O B E A H   H E N   T A B L E
R A T I O N A L I S A T I O N
S T A L W A R T   A L A T E D
E E L   E K E   C U L M
    I R R E S P O N S I B L E
S T A Y E D   U S A   A I L
H A T E D   W R Y   F A T A L
A L E   B O G   B A L E R S
M E D I C I N E B A L L S
    R A P T   E L S   M E N
C A S I N O   T A K E H O M E
O U T S I D E A G I T A T O R
P R E E N   A W L   T I E T O
T A W S E   U S E   O G L E S
```

98

```
L I N E D   O S H A     P O S H
A D O R E   L O O P   I M N O
P I R A T E S H I P   P A U L
I O S   E R O O   E N E R G Y
S T E P S O N   M A R C
    I T S   R O S A L I N D
M O L E S   D I V E   E S A U
A L A I   C O D E D   A I M S
N E O N   H O E S   I N S E T
N O S T R U M S   A C E
    H O T S   S T I R R U P
L O R E N Z   C H I C   U S E
A R E S   P I L O T L I G H T
M E E K   A V O N   E M B E R
B O D Y   H Y D E   S P Y R I
```

99

```
L A S H   E C H O   F A B L E
I N T O   T E A S   A F R O S
S T O C K H O L M   C R A P S
P I P K I N   L A C T A T E
    O I L   N A O M I
D A M A S C U S   C R E S T S
A W E E K   C A T H Y   L I E
M A X I   T A H O E   E A R N
E R I   V I S I T   E A V E S
S E C K E L   B E L G R A D E
    O N S E T   D U G
3 C I S S O R   N E G A T E
A L I V E   M O G A D I S H U
H O T E L   B L O C   N E A R
A B Y S S   S L A Y   N A T O
```

100

```
C E A S E L E S S   H A S P S
I N S U R A N C E   O R T H O
C A S S A N D R A   C A R O B
A M A   D U E T   B O N E
D E I S M   E E R   T Y L E R
A L L E Y S   C O C A   L I E
    A R T   H U R T   E N D
N A T I O N   T A T E R S
C A N   A N E W   M O A
U Z I   D E E R   P O R T A L
L A M A S   D E B   S L I M E
P R A M   L A R S   C P A
R E T I E   E T I O L A T E D
I T O L D   S H A R E W A R E
T H R E E   S E N T E N C E D
```